Leisure Guides

HERTFORDSHIRE

Leisure Guides

Kent by Pat Davis
Lancashire by Alan and Dorothy Sewart
Surrey by Valerie Porter

Leisure Guides

HERTFORDSHIRE

Jon Culverhouse

ROBERT HALE · LONDON

First published in Great Britain 1989

Robert Hale Limited
Clerkenwell House
Clerkenwell Green
London EC1R 0HT

British Library Cataloguing in Publication Data

Culverhouse, Jonathan, 1945–
Leisure guides : Hertfordshire (Leisure guides)
1. Hertfordshire. Visitors' guides
I. Title II. Series
914.25'804858

ISBN 0–7090–3826–7

Photoset in North Wales by
Derek Doyle & Associates, Mold, Clwyd.
Printed in Great Britain by
St Edmundsbury Press Ltd, Bury St Edmunds, Suffolk.
Bound by WBC Bookbinders Limited.

Contents

Acknowledgements

I would like to thank my sister Patsy and her husband George Walters for their invaluable and painstaking work in bringing this book to completion.

The help and advice received from the following are gratefully acknowledged:

The District Councils of Broxbourne, Dacorum, East Herts, Hertsmere, North Herts, St Albans, Stevenage, Three Rivers, Watford, Welwyn and Hatfield.

The Tourist Information Centres at Berkhamsted, Bishop's Stortford, Borehamwood, Hemel Hempstead, Hertford, Hitchin, Rickmansworth, St Albans, Stevenage, Welwyn Garden City.

Thanks are also due to Hertfordshire County Council; Tourist Marketing Officer, Herts County Council; Mr and Mrs Penney, Ringing Master and Secretary of the Abbey Ringers at St Albans; Mrs A.E. Woodall, County Organizer for Hertfordshire of the National Gardens Scheme; Mrs Stanley and Mrs Francis of the National Federation of Women's Institutes.

Maps

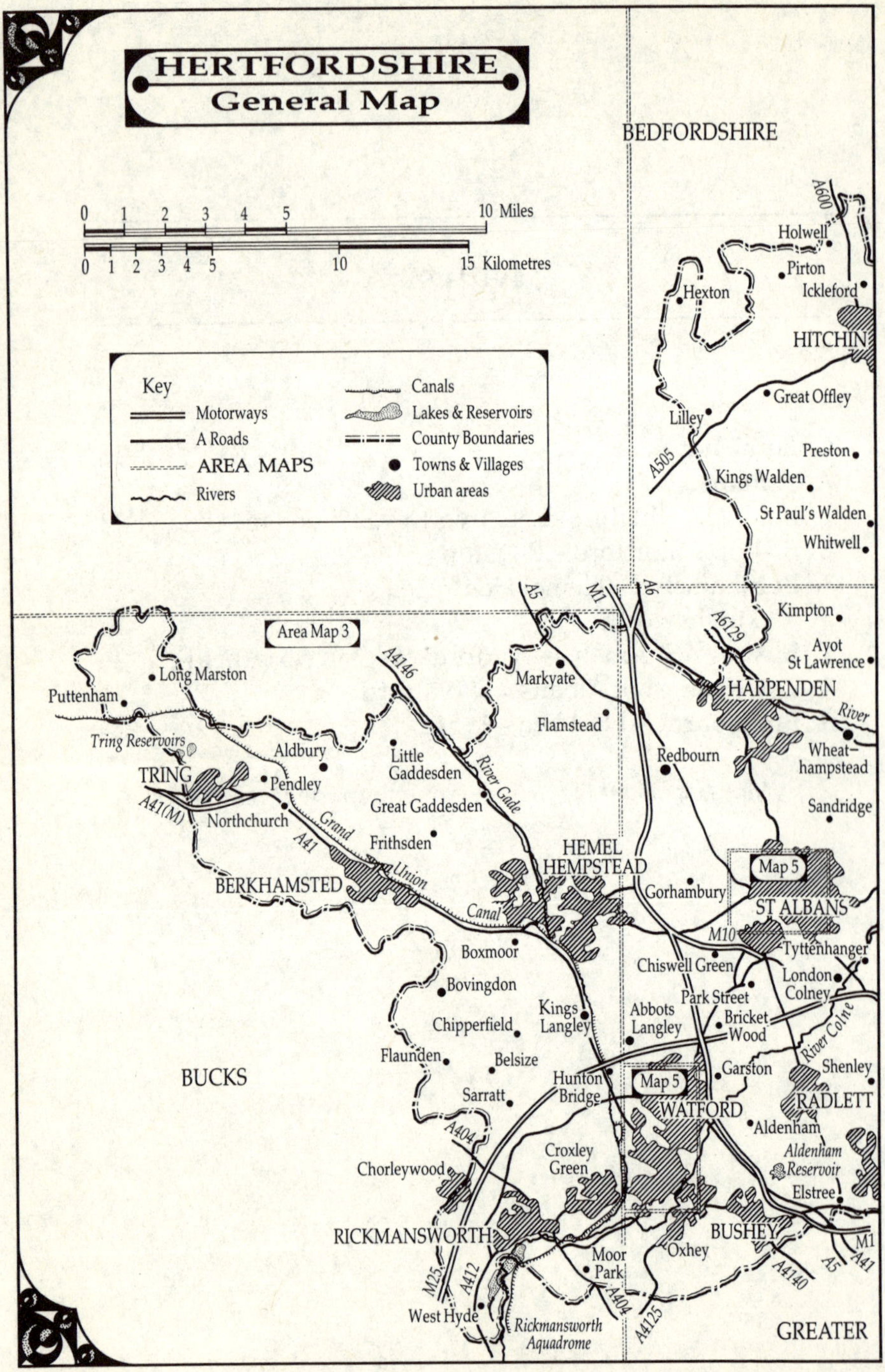
HERTFORDSHIRE
General Map
0 1 2 3 4 5 10 Miles
0 1 2 3 4 5 10 15 Kilometres
Key
Motorways
A Roads
AREA MAPS
Rivers
Canals
Lakes & Reservoirs
County Boundaries
Towns & Villages
Urban areas
BEDFORDSHIRE
BUCKS
GREATER
Area Map 3
Map 5
Map 5
A600
Holwell
Pirton
Ickleford
Hexton
HITCHIN
Great Offley
Lilley
A505
Preston
Kings Walden
St Paul's Walden
Whitwell
A5
M1
A6
A6129
Kimpton
Ayot St Lawrence
Long Marston
Puttenham
Tring Reservoirs
A4146
Markyate
Flamstead
HARPENDEN
River
Wheat-hampstead
Redbourn
Aldbury
Little Gaddesden
River Gade
TRING
Pendley
A41(M)
Northchurch
Great Gaddesden
Sandridge
Grand
A41
Frithsden
HEMEL HEMPSTEAD
BERKHAMSTED
Union
Canal
Gorhambury
ST ALBANS
M10
Boxmoor
Chiswell Green
Tyttenhanger
London Colney
Bovingdon
Park Street
Kings Langley
Abbots Langley
Bricket Wood
Chipperfield
River Colne
Flaunden
Belsize
Hunton Bridge
Garston
Shenley
Sarratt
WATFORD
RADLETT
A404
Aldenham
Aldenham Reservoir
Croxley Green
Chorleywood
Elstree
RICKMANSWORTH
BUSHEY
M1
Oxhey
Moor Park
A41
A5
A4140
M25
A412
A404
A4125
West Hyde
Rickmansworth Aquadrome

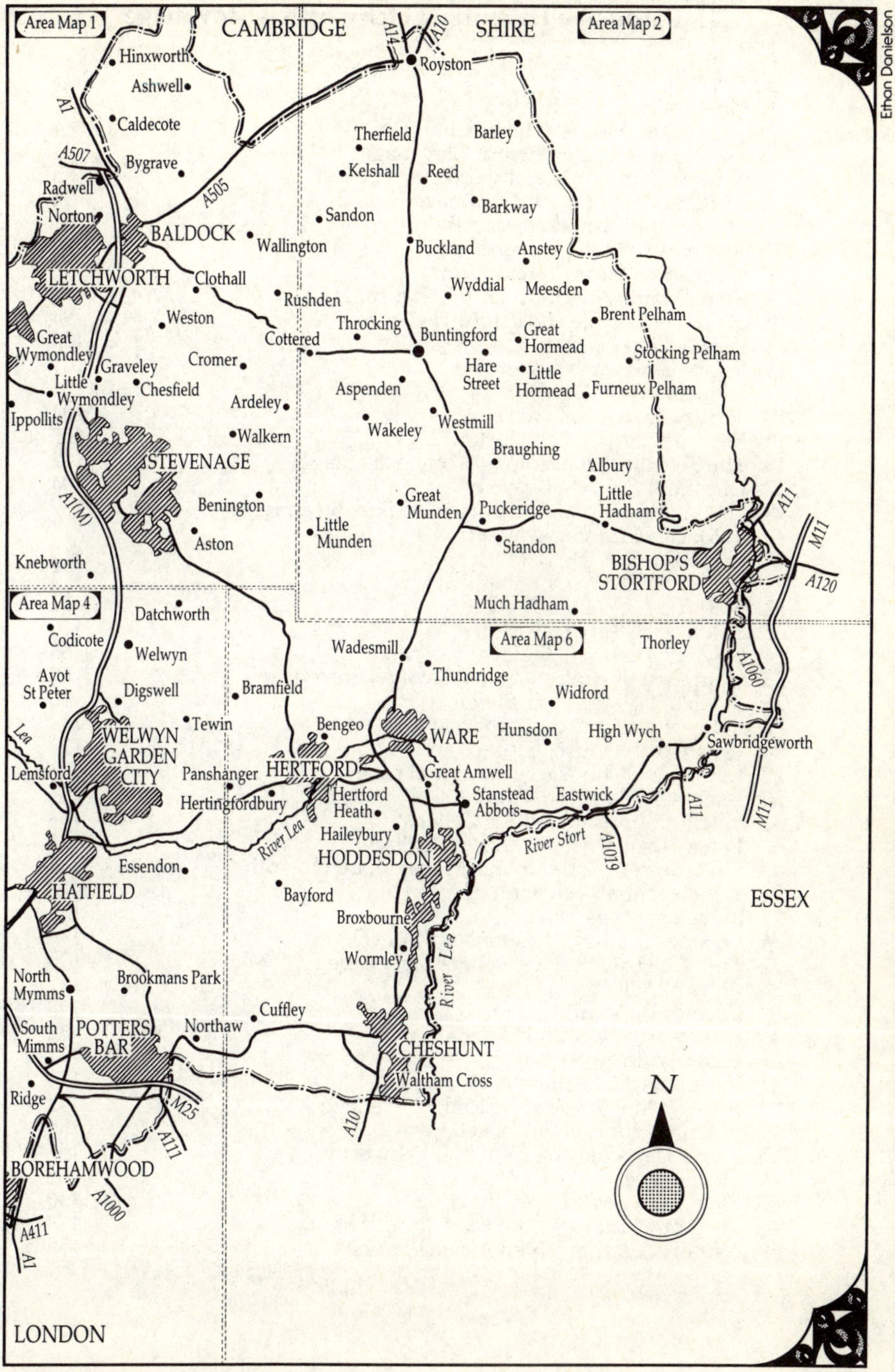

Area Map 1
CAMBRIDGE
SHIRE
Area Map 2
Hinxworth
Ashwell
Royston
A14
A10
A1
Caldecote
Therfield
Barley
A507
Bygrave
Kelshall
Reed
Radwell
A505
Barkway
Norton
Sandon
BALDOCK
Wallington
Buckland
Anstey
LETCHWORTH
Clothall
Wyddial
Meesden
Rushden
Brent Pelham
Weston
Throcking
Great Hormead
Stocking Pelham
Great Wymondley
Cottered
Buntingford
Cromer
Hare Street
Little Hormead
Graveley
Little Wymondley
Chesfield
Aspenden
Furneux Pelham
Ardeley
Ippollits
Westmill
Wakeley
Walkern
Braughing
STEVENAGE
Albury
A1(M)
Benington
Great Munden
Puckeridge
Little Hadham
A11
Little Munden
Aston
Standon
M11
Knebworth
BISHOP'S STORTFORD
A120
Area Map 4
Datchworth
Much Hadham
Codicote
Area Map 6
Thorley
Welwyn
Wadesmill
Thundridge
A1060
Ayot St Peter
Digswell
Bramfield
Widford
Lea
Tewin
Bengeo
WELWYN GARDEN CITY
Hunsdon
High Wych
WARE
Sawbridgeworth
HERTFORD
Great Amwell
Lemsford
Panshanger
Hertford Heath
Stanstead Abbots
Eastwick
Hertingfordbury
A11
M11
Haileybury
River Stort
River Lea
A1019
HODDESDON
Essendon
HATFIELD
ESSEX
Bayford
Broxbourne
Wormley
River Lea
North Mymms
Brookmans Park
Cuffley
South Mimms
POTTERS BAR
Northaw
CHESHUNT
Waltham Cross
N
Ridge
M25
A10
A111
BOREHAMWOOD
A1000
A411
A1
LONDON
Ethan Danielson

1. Baldock – Hitchin – Letchworth – Stevenage

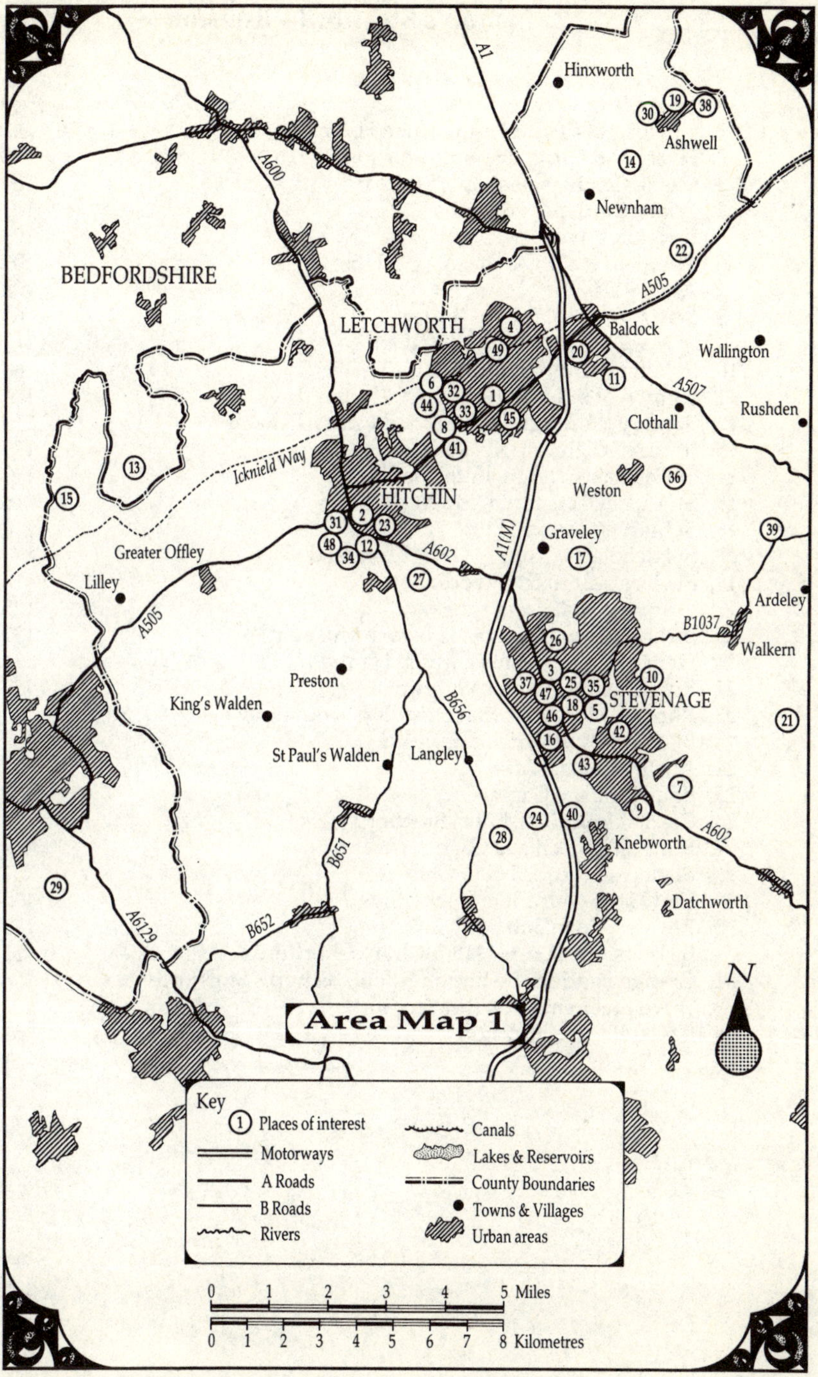

Area Map 1

Ethan Danielson

2. Bishop's Stortford – Royston

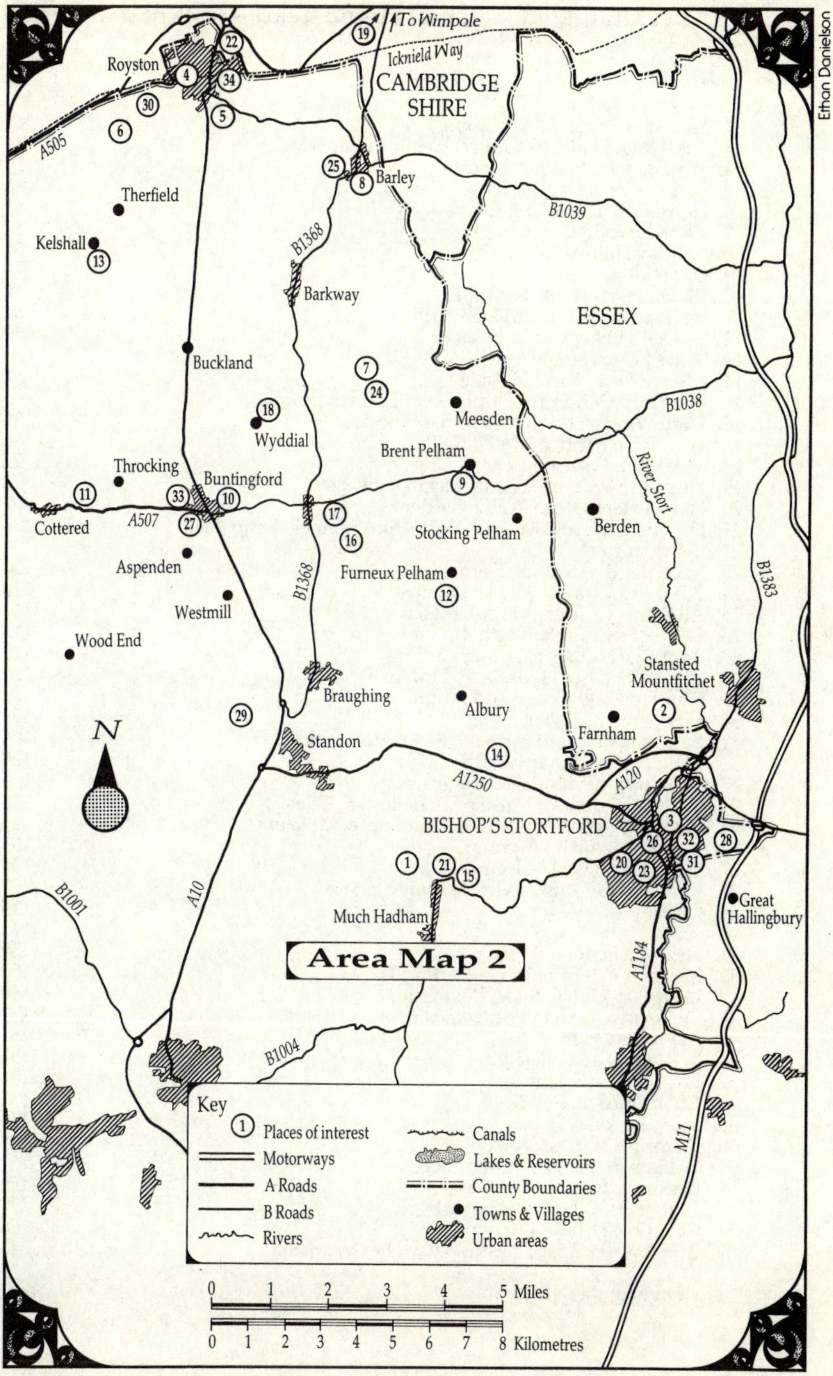
Area Map 2
Royston
CAMBRIDGE SHIRE
ESSEX
To Wimpole
Icknield Way
A505
Therfield
Kelshall
Barley
B1039
B1368
Barkway
Buckland
Meesden
B1038
Wyddial
Brent Pelham
Throcking
Buntingford
River Stort
Cottered
A507
Stocking Pelham
Berden
Aspenden
Furneux Pelham
B1383
Westmill
Wood End
Stansted Mountfitchet
Braughing
Albury
Farnham
Standon
A1250
A120
BISHOP'S STORTFORD
Great Hallingbury
Much Hadham
B1001
A10
A1184
B1004
M11
Key
Places of interest
Motorways
A Roads
B Roads
Rivers
Canals
Lakes & Reservoirs
County Boundaries
Towns & Villages
Urban areas
0 1 2 3 4 5 Miles
0 1 2 3 4 5 6 7 8 Kilometres
N
Ethan Danielson

3. Berkhamsted – Hemel Hempstead – Rickmansworth

* No longer open to the public

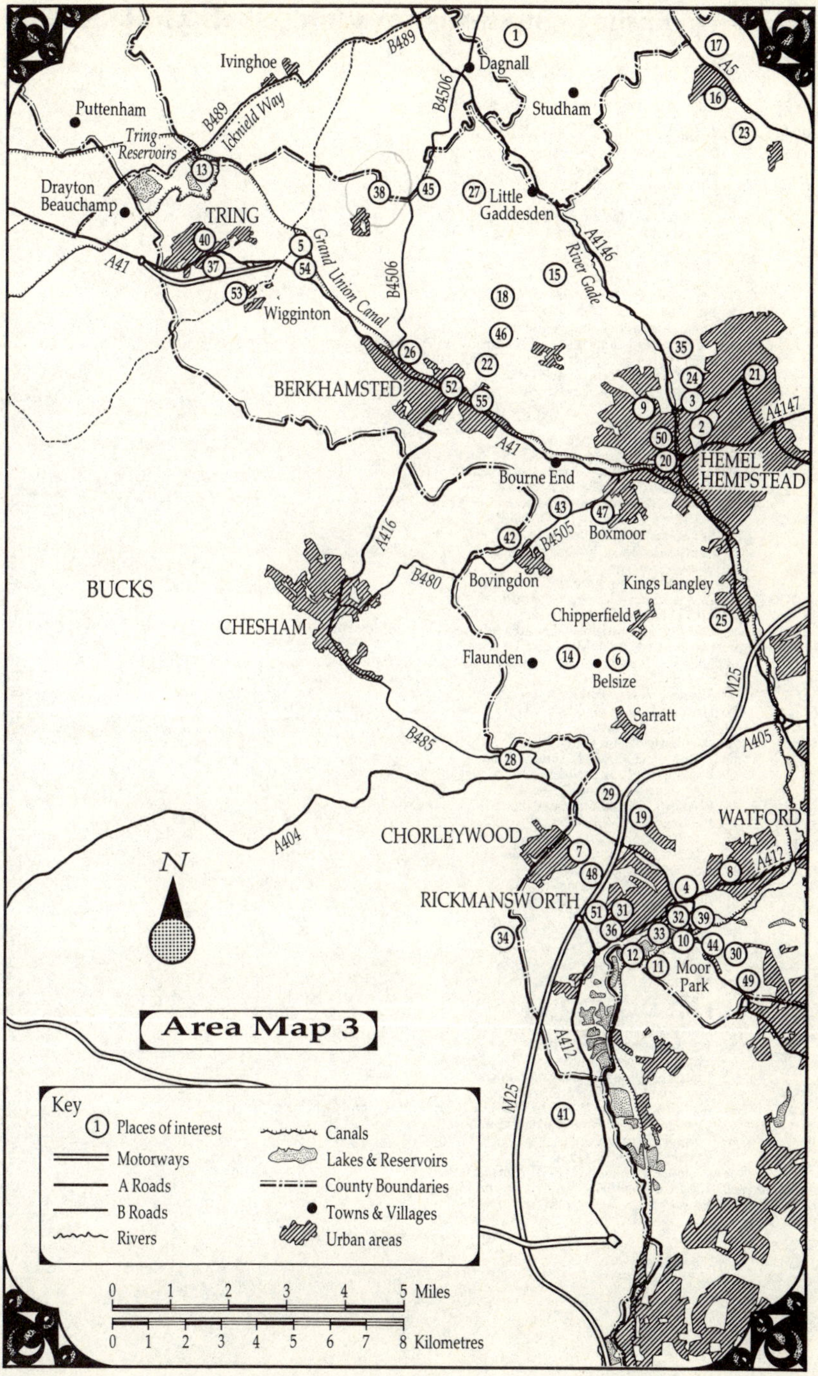

Ethan Danielson
Area Map 3
Ivinghoe
Dagnall
Studham
Puttenham
Tring Reservoirs
Icknield Way
Drayton Beauchamp
TRING
Little Gaddesden
Grand Union Canal
River Gade
Wigginton
BERKHAMSTED
HEMEL HEMPSTEAD
Bourne End
Boxmoor
Bovingdon
Kings Langley
Chipperfield
BUCKS
CHESHAM
Flaunden
Belsize
Sarratt
WATFORD
CHORLEYWOOD
RICKMANSWORTH
Moor Park
B489
B4506
A5
A41
A4146
A4147
A416
B4505
B480
B485
A404
A405
M25
A412
N
Key
Places of interest
Motorways
A Roads
B Roads
Rivers
Canals
Lakes & Reservoirs
County Boundaries
Towns & Villages
Urban areas
0 1 2 3 4 5 Miles
0 1 2 3 4 5 6 7 8 Kilometres

4. Bushey – St Albans – Watford – Welwyn/Hatfield

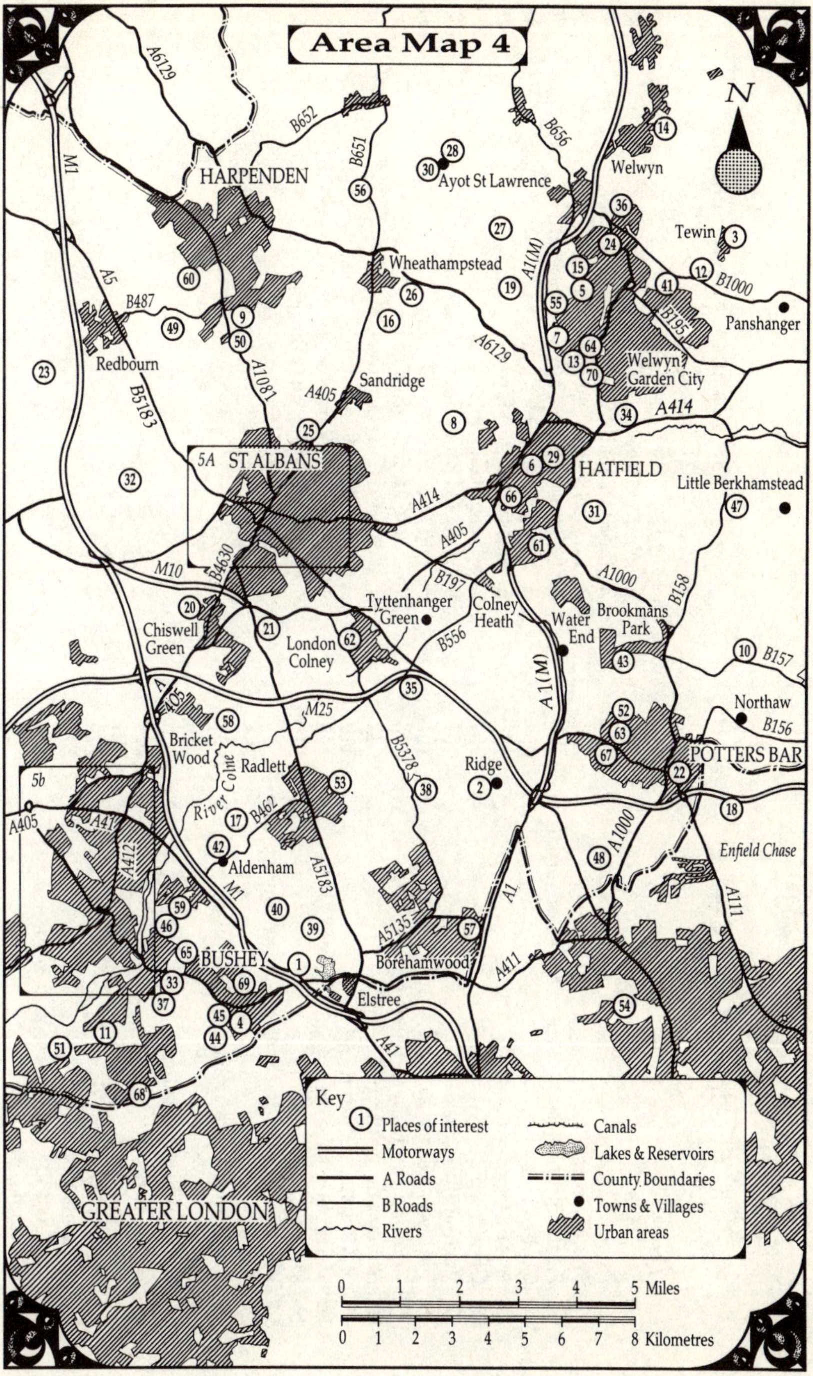

Ethan Danielson

5. St. Albans Town Centre

Location	Page
1. City Hall	42
2. Abbey Theatre	44
3. The Maltings	44
4. Herts and Middx Trust for Conservation, Grebe House	54
5. Abbey Orchard	101
6. Clarence Park	101
7. Verulamium Park	101
8. Vintry Gardens	101
9. Verulamium/Roman Theatre	106
10. Abbey and Cathedral	42
11. St Michael's Church	119
12. St Stephen's Church	119
13. Museum of St Albans	135
14. Westminster Lodge Sports Centre, Swimming-Pool	156
15. Kingsbury Watermill and Museum	135
16. Organ Museum	138
17. Verulamium Museum	138
18. Clock Tower	129
19. Fishpool Street	129
20. French Row	129
21. Sopwell Nunnery	129
22. Batchwood Golf Course and Tennis	151
23. Verulam Golf Club	153

5. Watford Town Centre

Location	Page
1. Watford Town Hall	43
2. Palace Theatre	45
3. Pump House Theatre	46
4. Cassiobury Park and Whippendell Woods	55
5. Ironbridge Lock	48
6. Cassiobridge Marina	48
7. Cheslyn Gardens	32
8. Watford Museum and Art Gallery	136
9. Old Free School	131
10. Leavesden Flight Centre	150
11. Watford Golf Driving-Range	153
12. West Herts Golf Club	153
13. Watford Leisure Centre, Woodside Park	156
14. Watford Swimming Baths	158
15. Leggatts Pool	158

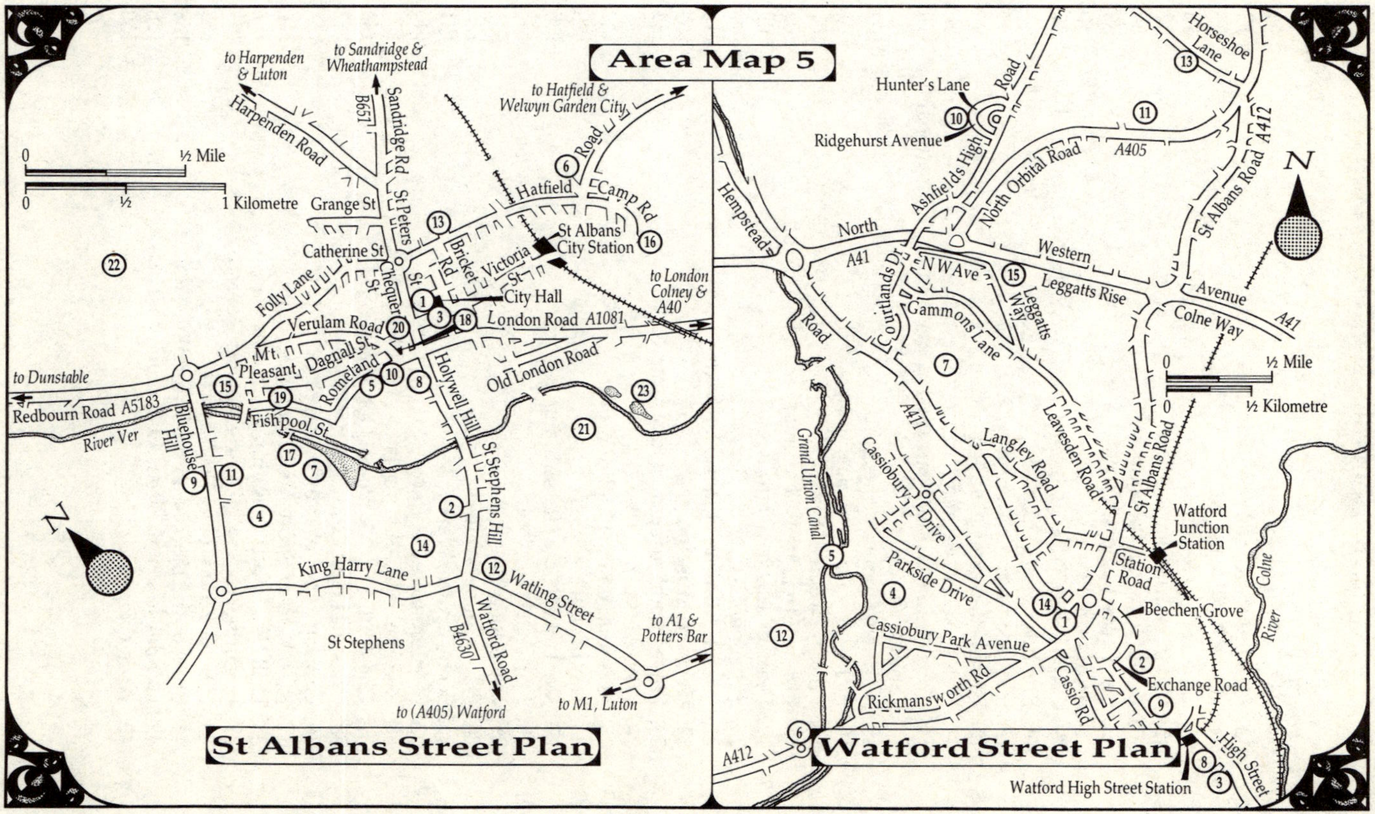
Area Map 5
St Albans Street Plan
Watford Street Plan
to Harpenden & Luton
to Sandridge & Wheathampstead
to Hatfield & Welwyn Garden City
to London Colney & A40
to Dunstable
to (A405) Watford
to M1, Luton
to A1 & Potters Bar
Harpenden Road
Sandridge Rd
B651
St Peters
Grange St
Hatfield Road
Camp Rd
St Albans City Station
Catherine St
Chequer St
St
Bricket Rd
Victoria St
City Hall
London Road A1081
Folly Lane
Verulam Road
Mt Pleasant
Dagnall St
Romeland
Holywell Hill
Old London Road
Redbourn Road A5183
River Ver
Bluehouse Hill
Fishpool St
St Stephens Hill
King Harry Lane
Watling Street
Watford Road
B4630
St Stephens
½ Mile
1 Kilometre
Hempstead Road
North Western Avenue
A41
Courtlands Dr
N W Ave
Leggatts Way
Leggatts Rise
Gammons Lane
Colne Way
Hunter's Lane
Ridgehurst Avenue
Ashfields High Road
North Orbital Road
A405
Horseshoe Lane
St Albans Road
A412
A411
Langley Road
Leavesden Road
Grand Union Canal
Cassiobury Drive
Parkside Drive
Cassiobury Park Avenue
Rickmansworth Rd
Cassio Rd
Watford Junction Station
Station Road
Beechen Grove
Exchange Road
High Street
Watford High Street Station
River Colne
½ Kilometre
Ethan Danielson

6. Broxbourne – Hertford – Ware

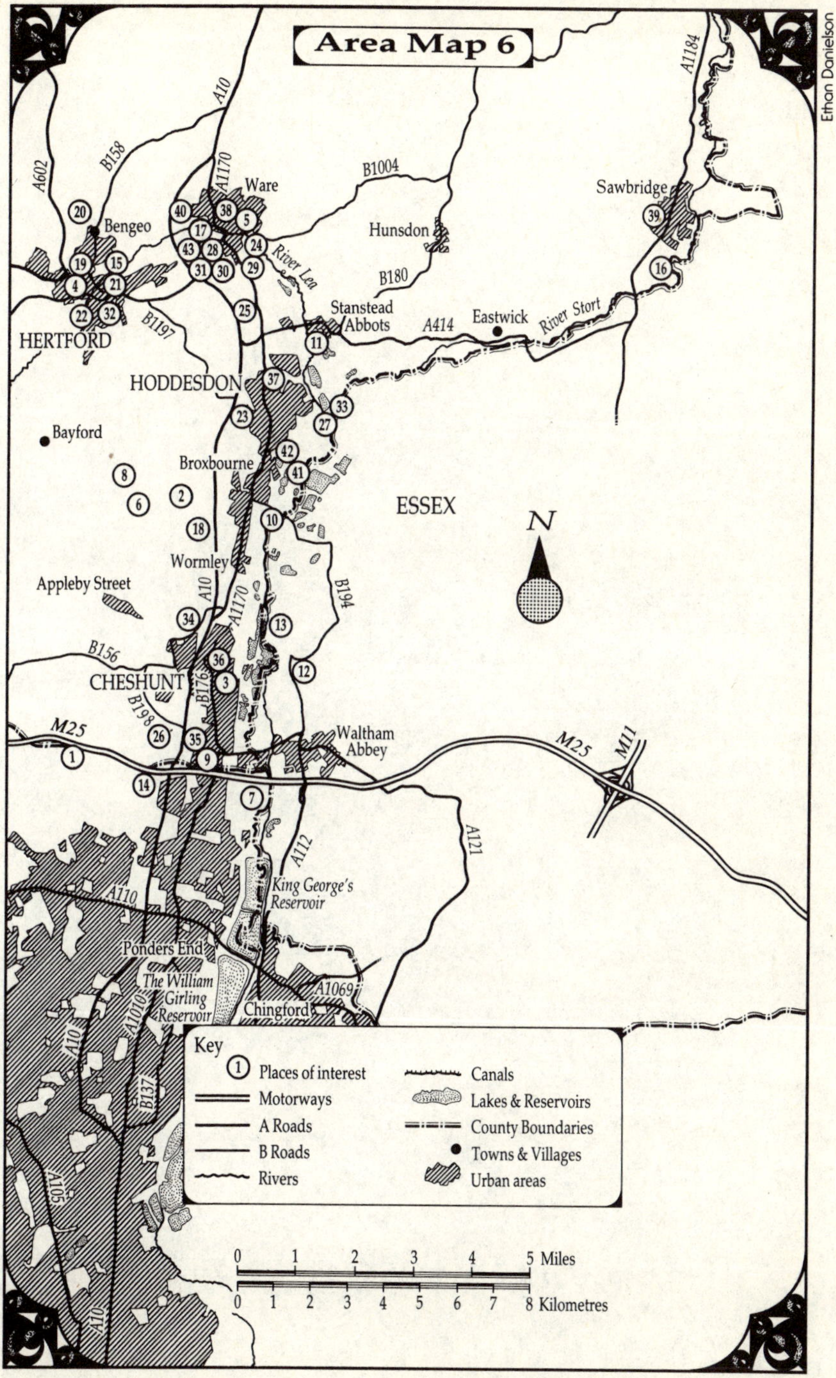
Area Map 6
Ethan Danielson
HERTFORD
Bengeo
Ware
Hunsdon
Sawbridge
Stanstead Abbots
Eastwick
HODDESDON
Bayford
Broxbourne
ESSEX
Wormley
Appleby Street
CHESHUNT
Waltham Abbey
King George's Reservoir
Ponders End
The William Girling Reservoir
Chingford
River Lea
River Stort
A10
A602
B158
A1170
B1004
B180
A414
A1184
B1197
B194
B156
B176
B198
M25
M11
A112
A121
A110
A1069
A1010
B137
A105
N
Key
Places of interest
Motorways
A Roads
B Roads
Rivers
Canals
Lakes & Reservoirs
County Boundaries
Towns & Villages
Urban areas
0 1 2 3 4 5 Miles
0 1 2 3 4 5 6 7 8 Kilometres

Introduction

The dictionary defines leisure as the freedom or opportunity to do something – more particularly the opportunity afforded by unoccupied time – and the enjoyment of this. The scope of this book is therefore enormous: all those things which people find to do in their spare time in order to enjoy themselves – exploration of town and country, whether on foot or by car or cycle or bus or train or navigable waterway; all forms of sport; enjoyment of the arts; shopping; eating and drinking etc. However, the compass of the book is, by design, comparatively small, and so it follows that it does not pretend to be a complete guide. Rather is it a series of signposts pointing the way, enabling the reader to find out more for himself and, where appropriate, suggesting other – and fuller – sources of information and guidance in particular fields.

At times the guide crosses the boundary into other counties. For example, it includes entries on Whipsnade Zoo, Luton Hoo, Wimpole Hall and Chiltern Open Air Museum. In each such case, the item is a major attraction in its own field and so close to the county boundary that it would be pedantic to exclude it.

Different maps are required for different purposes. If you are walking, the relevant sheet of the Ordnance Survey Pathfinder Series (1:25 000 or about 2½ inches to 1 mile) is a boon, as it shows all the public rights of way, but if you are motoring, a small scale is better. A useful all-purpose map is Sheet 15 of Bartholomew's National Map Series (1:100 000 or about 1.6 miles to 1 inch), which covers the whole of Herts and Bucks (and bits of contiguous counties) on one sheet.

A select list of further reading is included as an appendix, but in those cases where it is helpful to do so, specific reference is made to particular books in the body of the text.

Finally, there are brief introductions to a number of chapters either to explain the basis of selection of the various items or to clarify the procedure adopted. If, by any chance, important aspects of leisure in the county have been omitted, the plea in mitigation is that which Dr Johnson offered as his explanation of error: pure ignorance! Every effort has been made to be accurate, but things are constantly changing, and so this book should be treated as a guide not a bible.

Abbreviations

BD = Boxing Day
BH = Bank Holiday
BHM = Bank Holiday Monday
D = A part, but not necessarily all, of the site is suitable for the disabled, or there are special facilities (toilets, wheelchair hire). The absence of that sign does not, however, mean that access is entirely impracticable.
E = Easter
EH = English Heritage
GF = Good Friday
LT = London Transport
NCC = Nature Conservancy Council
NT = National Trust
NYD = New Year's Day
P = Parking
RSPB = Royal Society for the Protection of Birds
XD = Christmas Day

Animals and Birds

AQUATIC LIFE, AVIARIES AND WILDLIFE

See also Hoddesdon: Lowewood Museum and Stevenage Museum in Heritage: Museums.

Aldenham: Aldenham Reservoir and Country Park
Dagger Lane, Elstree (01 953 9602)
Well signposted from the A5, A41 and M1 (junction 5). LT bus 107 from Edgware Station or Elstree & Borehamwood Station to Elstree village. From Watford or Borehamwood use London Country Bus service 306 to the Fishery Inn.

P (fee)

The general attractions of Aldenham Country Park are described in Countryside: Country Parks. This entry deals with the special collection of animals at the park. They are all domestic animals in the sense that they were all bred to provide man with food. As a result of changing tastes and farming methods, some are now rare breeds, and so a visit to the park offers a good opportunity to see these endangered species. A major part of the collection is a herd of the famous Longhorn cattle. Other interesting breeds include British Saanen goats, British Toggenburg goats, Old English pheasant fowl and many other types of hens, ducks and geese, together with English and Dutch rabbits. All the animals have special diets, and at certain times you can feed them with food bought from park staff. However, please do not feed any animal without supervision by a park ranger.

Daily: May–August: Tuesday–Sunday, 9–8; Monday, 10–8. September–April: 9–dusk.

Enfield, Middx: Enfield Butterfly Centre

Cattlegate Road, Crews Hill, Enfield, Middx (01 363 7288) P

Next to Crews Hill Station. It can easily be reached from junction 25 on the M25. The collection is probably one of the finest in the Home Counties, and many unusual and spectacular types of butterfly can be seen flying freely in the tropical garden. Large gift shop selling souvenirs and unusual gifts. Don't forget your camera.

Schools and organized parties are always welcome, but please book in advance. It is possible to combine a visit to the Butterfly Centre with a tour of the garden centres at Forty Hall or Capel Manor Educational Farm (see Farms) and a composite educational package has been devised for school parties. For those with lots of energy, the White Webbs Nature Trail is only a short walk from the centre.

Daily: March–October, 9.30–6; November–February, 10–4.

Fee

Markyate: Woodside Farm and Wild Fowl Park

Mancroft Road, Aley Green, near Slip End, Markyate, Beds (0582 841044) P

The wildlife aspects of this establishment are covered in the Farms chapter.

All year: Monday–Saturday, from 9.30. Closing times vary according to time of year and weather conditions.

Much Hadham: Gingercress Trout Farm

027984 2225

The lovely village of Much Hadham stands in the Ash valley between Ware and Bishop's Stortford, and the trout farm is on the outskirts of the village. P

It is a working fish farm and fishery, set in 20 unspoilt acres. You can either buy trout or try your hand at catching them yourself from the lake. Carp fishing is also on offer. There is a nature trail and picnic and barbecue area. Ornamental fish and water lilies are also to be seen, and there is a 'dipping' pond which gives children an opportunity to identify pond life. As well as a farm shop, there is a display of wetland wildlife and an exhibition centre.

Daily: 10-6 (or dusk). Fee for some activities

Ridge: RSPCA Animal Centre

Packhorse Lane, Southridge (0707 42153) P

You can see birds of prey, goats, rabbits, cats and dogs at this animal centre, and it is a good place to choose a new pet. Donation

Tewin: Tewin Mill Fish Farm and Water Gardens

Kingsbridge, Tewin, Welwyn (043871 6019)

Between Hertford and Welwyn on the B1000. P

Landscaped ponds and water gardens set in 15 acres of land. Tropical and marine fish. Coldwater fish. Ornamental fish from all over the world, including koi, fancy goldfish and farm-bred fish. Aquatic plants, lilies, pond-liners and everything for the water garden. Trout and fish farm: feeding-times noon and 2 p.m. Flyfishing lake. Catch your own trout . Reptile house and exhibition of exotic birds.

Daily: 9–5.30.

Watford: Cheslyn Gardens

Nascot Wood Road, Watford (0923 226400, ext. 2501)

There is an aviary in these gardens (see Gardens) with 14 different types of birds.

Aviary: May–September, Friday–Wednesday, 10–8. October, November, Friday–Wednesday, 10–4. (Except XD, BD.)

ZOO PARKS

Broxbourne: Paradise Park and Woodland Zoo
White Stubbs Lane, Broxbourne (0992 468001)
Clearly signposted from Broxbourne. P
This small (25-acre) zoo contains a wide variety of mostly small animals – some of which roam freely in the park. They include Bobby, the famous African lion born at the zoo, Minnie, the Vietnamese pot-bellied pig, and her companion Blue Bell, llama, wallabies, Shetland ponies, goats, rhea, sheep, rabbits, donkeys and a variety of birds – peacocks, pheasant, doves and bantams. A recent addition is an aviary containing eagle owls. A small-gauge woodland railway traverses the western wood, and there are ample picnic spots, children's playground facilities and refreshment/dining-rooms. D (toilets)/Fee
Daily: 10–5 or dusk.

Dunstable, Beds: Whipsnade Zoological Park
(0582 872171) P
Off the M1, junction 9, or off the A5 near Markyate.
Opened in 1931 by the then Zoological Society of London (now the Royal Zoological Society) as a country home for animals of London Zoo, Whipsnade Zoo is now very much a zoo in its own right. Indeed, it has served as a model for many of the world's finest, with most of the animals kept not in cages but in open paddocks and compounds around the 500-acre park in the Chiltern Hills high over Dunstable. Among the collection of more than 2,000 animals are old-established favourites such as elephants, sea-lions, tigers, bears, chimpanzees, spider monkeys and hippos. But you can also see some rare breeds – Przewalski's wild horses and Siberian tigers. There is a dolphinarium where bottle-nosed dolphins perform their engaging routines daily. (They can be watched also from the viewing-gallery below the indoor pool.) A narrow-gauge safari railway passes through the

30-acre white rhino compound. There is a special children's zoo, where ponies, sheep and goats wander at will. Next to the children's zoo is a playground, and also nearby an area where pony rides are available during the summer months. The zoo's education department will make special provision for schools, offering programmes of talks and tours on request.

A visit to Whipsnade is a full day out. You can either bring a picnic or take advantage of the refreshment facilities available. If you don't feel like walking all the way round, you may drive round for an extra charge. Fee

Daily: Monday–Saturday, 10–6; Sunday and BHs, 10–7 (or dusk).

Railway: Fine afternoons Easter–September, winter weekends and most school holidays.

Arts and Crafts

ART CENTRES AND GALLERIES

For other art galleries, see Heritage: Museums.

Barnet: Old Bull Arts Centre
High Street, Barnet (01 449 5189) P
This is a lively and extensive centre, having 2 theatres, an art and craft gallery and craft workshops. There are many activities especially for children, including classes and workshops. A children's show is produced every fortnight, and a children's theatre runs ever Sunday at 3 p.m. A children's festival is held every summer.

Bushey: Lucy Kemp-Welch Memorial Gallery
(01 950 3240)
On the first floor of Church House, next to the parish church of St James. This exhibition is of paintings by artists living or working in Bushey, and paintings of places in Bushey or local scenes and people. Works owned by the Bushey Museum Trust are also exhibited.
Saturday, 10.30–noon.

Cheshunt: Wolsey Hall
Windmill Lane, Cheshunt (0992 28567/32812) P
The main hall seats 400 and a smaller hall 100. Concerts, films and dinner dances are held here, and it is a good

venue for conferences, exhibitions and club meetings. Bar, leisure shop. D

Hemel Hempstead: Old Town Hall Arts Centre

High Street, Hemel Hempstead (0442 64451)

This is a Victorian building in a Jacobean style with an open-pillared ground floor from which you can look down into the churchyard. It was once the centre for civic affairs but is now the venue for small-scale professional drama, dance and mime events. From September to May the Arts Centre presents shows for children on alternate Saturdays. It incorporates a studio and art gallery and stages photographic and art exhibitions, recitals and folk and jazz clubs. The cellar is completely refurbished, and weekly folk and rock-on record clubs are held.

Hertford: Castle Hall

The Castle, Hertford (0279 55261, ext. 487)

This big hall next to the ruins of the castle offers a full programme of events and entertainment for all: cinema club, wrestling, auctions, craft fairs, concerts, tea dances, whist drives, operatic and dramatic society presentations. The River Room Suite, in a picturesque setting overlooking the Old Mill Race, is available for hire. Bar.

Letchworth: Plinston Hall

Broadway, Letchworth (0462 672003)

This is a modern, compact and versatile centre for community leisure. It has air-conditioning and is well appointed and equipped. It has theatrical and other stage presentations, displays, exhibitions, film shows demonstrations, talks, lectures and a variety of indoor sporting events (see Sport). It is an ideal venue for meetings, lunches, receptions and dinner dances. The Gardens Gallery, comfortably furnished, has a pleasant view overlooking Kennedy Gardens. Large stage with ambitious lighting, dressing-rooms, mothers' and toddlers' group, discos, chess, beekeepers society, slimming groups, bridge club, yoga, art club, healing meetings, new photographic studio service.

Rickmansworth: Watersmeet

High Street, Rickmansworth (0923 771542)

The modern entertainments centre named after the 3 rivers that meet – the Chess, the Colne and the Gade – hosts a wide variety of events and entertainments. The Gade Theatre is the venue for theatre productions, cinema, concerts, ballets, discos, dances, exhibitions, markets and productions by amateur and touring companies. The Chess Suite and the Colne Suite are also available for hire and offer facilities to business and the local community for meetings, seminars and conferences, and for wedding receptions.

Welwyn Garden City: Campus West

(0707 332880) P

This purpose-built entertainment complex has a theatre which is used for productions by local operatic and dramatic societies, and shows a varied programme of films. An improvement programme has established superb facilities for roller-skating in the Exhibition Hall. The complex has been adapted to form a venue for a wide variety of events such as flower shows, trade shows, seminars, conferences, exhibitions and antique fairs. The banqueting suites cater for functions seating up to 350 people. Concerts, recitals and pantomimes. Cafeteria. Changing-rooms. Information point.

BELL-RINGING

Many churches have bells which are rung before services by a team of ringers. They are led by a ringing master or tower captain. The exercise that you have when ringing a bell is as good as any weight-training session. If you are interested in joining a team of bell-ringers, you should contact your local church and ask for the telephone number of the bell-ringers' secretary.

The different patterns of pulling the bells have been given names, such as Plain Hunt, Bob Major and Grandsire Triple. In 1779 Braughing Youths rang a complete peal of 12,240 Bob Majors only 34 years after the first peal was ever rung there. In the church there is a day every year when this achievement is commemorated.

On 15 January 1989 in Tring, the 8 bells were rededicated after being tuned and rehung with mainly new fittings.

St Albans Abbey

To reach the bell chamber of St Albans Abbey, you have to climb 160 steps to get to the ringing chamber, which is 102 feet from the nave below. There are summer tours of the Abbey Tower and bells at St Albans Cathedral. If you would like to join a tour and go up to the ringing chamber, or if you would like to join the team of ringers there, you should contact the ringing master (0727 65276).

BRASS-RUBBING

Brass-rubbing is taking impressions on paper of memorials in brass. These are usually found in churches, either on the walls or more often lying flat in the aisles. Many churches are kept locked because of theft and vandalism but the key is usually obtainable from the vicarage or the verger. A charge is sometimes made for the facility. The following is a list of the churches in Hertfordshire that have fine brasses.

Asterisks denote that churches are described in the chapter Heritage: Churches, sometimes with a note on their brasses.

Abbots Langley: St Lawrence
Albury: St Mary
Aldbury: St John the Baptist
Aldenham: St John the Baptist
Ardeley: St Lawrence
Aspenden: St Mary
Aston: St Mary
*Baldock: St Mary the Virgin**
Barkway: St Mary Magdalene
Barley: St Margaret
Bayford: St Mary
*Benington: St Peter**
*Berkhamsted: St Peter**
Boxmoor: St John
Braughing: St Mary
*Brent Pelham: St Mary**
Broxbourne: St Augustine
Buckland: St Andrew
Buntingford: St Peter
Cheshunt: St Mary
Clothall: St Mary the Virgin
Digswell: St John the Evangelist
Eastwick: St Botolph
Essenden: St Mary
*Flamstead: St Leonard**
*Furneaux Pelham: St Mary the Virgin**
Great Amwell: St John the Baptist
Great Gaddesden: St John the Baptist
Harpenden: St Nicholas
Hatfield Hyde: St Mary Magdalene
*Hemel Hempstead: Great St Mary**
Hinxworth: St Nicholas
Hitchin: Holy Saviour
*Hitchin: St Mary**
Holywell: St Peter
Hunsdon: St Dunstan
Ickleford: St Katherine

Kelshall: St Faith
Kimpton: St Peter and St Paul
King's Langley: All Saints*
Letchworth: St Mary
Little Hadham: St Cecilia*
Much Hadham: St Andrew*
Nettleden: St Lawrence
Newnham: St Vincent
Northchurch: St Mary*
North Mymms: St Mary
Offley: St Mary Magdalene
Old Knebworth: St Mary
Redbourn: St Mary
Rickmansworth: St Mary the Virgin
Royston: St John
St Albans Cathedral*
St Albans: St Michael*
St Albans: St Peter
St Albans: St Stephen*
St Ippolyts: St Ippolyts*
Sandon: All Saints
Sawbridgeworth: Great St Mary
Shenley: St Martin
Standon: St Mary
Stanstead Abbots: St James
Stevenage: St Nicholas
Tewin: St Peter
Walkern: St Mary
Ware: St Mary
Wareside: Holy Trinity
Watford: St Mary and St James
Watton-at-Stone: St Andrew and St Mary
Wheathampstead: St Helen
Wormley: St Lawrence
Wyddial: St Giles*

For further information see *Hertfordshire Brasses* by Mary

Renston (Hertfordshire Publications, 1982), obtainable from Hertfordshire Library Service/Herts Local History Service, c/o East Division Library Headquarters, 38 High Street, Stevenage Old Town, Herts.

This book, which is probably available at your local library, not only tells you about the brasses to be found in the churches listed but also gives details of other useful publications about brass-rubbing and of centres where you learn how to do it. (Unfortunately there are no such centres in Hertfordshire itself.)

CINEMAS

Recent years have seen a sharp decline in the number of cinemas. The list which follows includes some which are not purpose-built cinemas, used for the sole purpose of showing films, but civic halls which periodically show films as well as other forms of entertainment.

Barnet: Odeon
(01 449 4147)
Borehamwood: Hertsmere Centre
(01 953 9872) Films from time to time.
Broxbourne: Civic Hall
High Street, Hoddesdon (0992 441946)
Hemel Hempstead: Odeon Marlowes
(0442 64013)
Hertford: Castle Cinema
Castle Hall (0992 589024/5)
Letchworth: Broadway Cinema
(0462 684721)
Potters Bar: The Oakmere Cinema
High Street (0707 45005)
Rickmansworth: Watersmeet
High Street (0923 771542) Films from time to time
Royston: Priory Cinema
(0763 243133)

St Albans: Odeon
London Road (0727 53888)
Stevenage: Cannon Cinemas
(0438 313267)
Waltham Cross: Cannon Cinemas
High Street (0992 761044)
Watford: Cannon Cinemas
Merton Road (0923 224088)

MUSIC

Hemel Hempstead: The Pavilion
Marlowes (0442 64451)
This is the main venue for indoor entertainment in Hemel Hempstead. Concerts given by famous orchestras and soloists take place here, as do plays, Christmas shows, pop music, recitals, wrestling and club nights. Bar, refreshments.

St Albans: City Hall
Off St Peter's Street (0727 44488)
Regular concerts – classical, pop and folk – and variety shows are held here. It is also the venue for live shows, films and discos. There are programmes of entertainments for the holidays, and the hall is available for private hire. Tea dances, ballets, celebrity speakers, wrestling. Bar.

St Albans: The Cathedral and Abbey Church
(0727 60780)
The beautiful Cathedral and Abbey Church of St Albans provides an excellent venue for organ recitals, choral events and other musical performances. The International Organ Festival is held here biennially (1989, 1991 etc).

Ware: Maltings Arts Centre
Kibes Lane, Ware
Ware Folk Club, the Jazz Club and the Maltings Sinfonia are among the groups who perform here.

Watford: Town Hall
(0923 226400) P
The town hall in Watford has fine acoustics, and top orchestras are engaged for regular seasons of concerts. The hall is sometimes used by recording companies for recording sessions. Popular weekly dances are also held.

Do you play a musical instrument? Can you sing? Why not join one of the numerous local choral or music societies and enjoy making music with other people. Most societies are glad to have new members. A list of local societies can be obtained from your district council or local library. Most music societies give concerts, sometimes to clubs, sometimes in churches or village halls and sometimes in town halls.

Both Hatfield and Watford boast a Philharmonic Orchestra and a Philharmonic Choir.

If you feel that your playing ability is not good enough for you to join one of these organizations, why not take advantage of enrolling for lessons at the Watford School of Music (Nascot Wood Road). This is one of the few schools of music in the county and is run by Hertfordshire County Council. The teaching staff are widely experienced professional musicians, and the students put on concerts both in the school's own recital hall and in the town hall. Many well-known musicians have started their careers at the school. (Tel: 0923 225531.)

THEATRES

Hatfield: Forum Theatre
(07072 71217)
Next to Hatfield swimming-pool. The Forum Theatre seats 750 people and has a warm and intimate atmosphere. Some of the most famous people in British and American show-business have appeared here. Regular screenings of films. Exhibitions in the foyer.

Hitchin: Queen Mother Theatre

Woodside, Walsworth Road, Hitchin (0462 55166)

In the heart of Hitchin, this new theatre offers shows and films for all ages. An appeal launched in 1982 for funds to build a theatre raised £111,000, and the Queen Mother opened it in 1983. It is the home of the Bancroft Players, the district's leading amateur dramatic society. Many leading professional artists have performed here. The auditorium has flexible staging and seats 200. Exhibition area and separate rehearsal studio. The Hunting Gate Bar is open weekday evenings, weekend lunchtimes and during performances.

St Albans: Abbey Theatre

Holywell Hill, St Albans (0727 57861)

The Abbey Theatre is owned by the Company of Ten. Apart from a brief summer break, a resident amateur company and other local amateur companies give performances of plays by a wide variety of writers from all over the world.

St Albans: The Maltings

(0727 444488)

Level 5 of the Maltings shopping complex. P

The Maltings consists of a sound-proof studio room and a main hall (900 square feet) which can be sectioned off into 3 smaller rooms or converted into a studio theatre. Foyer exhibitions, recitals by well-known artists and musicians, lecture recitals, children's theatre groups, craft fairs, local dramatic and music societies' productions. D

Open weekdays, 9.30–5.

Stevenage: Gordon Craig Theatre

Lytton Way, Stevenage (0438 316291)

This theatre, built to West End standards, was opened in 1975 and is part of the Stevenage Leisure Centre. It has 507 seats and was named after Edward Henry Gordon Craig

(1872–1966), the son of the distinguished actress Dame Ellen Terry and the architect Edwin William Godwin. Gordon Craig was born in Stevenage and was an actor, editor, publisher, author, theatre designer and producer. Other facilities at the centre include fully equipped studios, exhibition areas, rehearsal room, music room and scenery and wardrobe workshops. From September to April there are regular Saturday shows for children. The theatre organizes some children's shows during half-term and other holidays. Bars, cafeteria, children's toy library and crêche.

Tring: Pendley Arts Centre
(044282 2483)
There used to be a whole village on the site of this arts centre, but it was deserted in the 15th century after the owner, Sir Robert Whittingham, enclosed the land. The manor was rebuilt in Jacobean style in 1674. The late Dorian Williams, the well-known show-jumping commentator, was responsible for its development as a Residential Centre for Adult Education in 1945. Pendley Arts Centre is part of the centre, and during the Shakespeare Festival 2 plays are performed under floodlights on the lawns. The 30 acres of land in the park are available to local sports clubs.

Watford: Palace Theatre
Clarendon Road, Watford (0923 35455/225671)
The Palace Theatre is an attractive Edwardian building erected in 1908 as a music hall. It seats about 700 people and in 1965 became a civic theatre and is administered by a trust. It is the only professional theatre in Hertfordshire and presents a wide range of productions starring international actors and actresses. It has been the testing-ground for many new West End productions, which critics from the national press often review. Over the past few years the theatre has played on average to 90

per cent capacity, making it 'the most successful regional theatre in Britain'. Bars, refreshments.

Watford: Pump House Theatre and Arts Trust Ltd
Local Board Road, Watford (0923 220230)
The Pump House was built in 1854 to house the first water-supply scheme in Watford. The premises were leased from Watford Borough Council in 1971 to provide a theatre for amateur clubs and cultural activities. It is under the control of a trust, and its premises contain excellent facilities for all forms of artistic activity including drama, folk music, jazz and pop entertainment. 7 flourishing clubs operate from the Pump House: theatre, folk singing, women's and men's morris dancing, jazz and keep-fit. Ask to see the double-bass instrument made by a local resident, Herbert Walters, from a sycamore tree and now used as a prop.
For further information on clubs, production dates and programmes contact: The Chairman of the Trust, 79 Rickmansworth Road, Watford (0923 220230)

Welwyn Garden City: Barn Theatre
Handside Lane.
A small playhouse used by the Barn Theatre Club for plays and other productions. Youth Drama Festival held every May.

Countryside

BOAT TRIPS

There are two main waterways in Hertfordshire – the Grand Union Canal which, in the county, runs from Bulbourne near Tring to Rickmansworth (and thence to the Thames at Brentford), and the Lee & Stort Navigation, which runs from Limehouse in London's East End via Waltham Cross to Hertford and Bishop's Stortford, dividing into 2 parts at Fielde's Weir, Hoddesdon. Both systems were at one time highly important commercial waterways, but they are now mainly for leisure and recreation. Have you thought of combining a river cruise with visits to some of the interesting places *en route*? The operational centres and sources of detailed information are as follows:

Broxbourne: Broxbourne Boat Centre
Part of Lee Valley Regional Park (see Countryside: Country Parks). 0992 462085 for leaflet giving details of prices and timings.
Leave the A10 at the A1170 Broxbourne exit; proceed to town centre; turn down Station Road, and the Boat Centre is on the right after crossing the viaduct. An easy walk from Broxbourne Station.
Small boats and 8-seater electric boats available for hire, and 45-foot narrowboats for family holidays. 52-seater waterbus *Pride of Lee* runs on Sundays and BHs

Easter–October, and Monday–Thursday (and some Fridays) during school summer holidays.

Stanstead Abbots: Marina
In South Street, Stanstead Abbots.
Part of the Lee Valley Regional Park (see Countryside: Country Parks). 0920 870499 for details of facilities available.

GRAND UNION CANAL

Berkhamsted; Bridgewater Boats (M. & L. Foster) Ltd
Castle Wharf, Bridge Street, Berkhamsted (044 27 3615)
Narrow boats for daily or weekly hire.

Tring: Cow Roast Marina
Cow Roast, Tring (9044 282 3222)
Narrowboats for hire on a weekly basis only.

Watford: 'Arcturus' narrowboat trips
Ironbridge Lock in Cassiobury Park, Watford. Bookings and information: 043871 4528.
Public trips: Easter-October, Sunday, 2.30 and 4 p.m. as required; in August also Tuesday and Thursday, 2 and 3.30 p.m. Fee

Watford: Cassio Bridge Marina Ltd
Cassio Bridge, Watford (0923 49158)
Moorings for private craft.
Canoeing and rowing are allowed on the canal, provided the boats are licensed. Licences and navigation certificates may be obtained from the British Waterways Board, Willow Grange, Watford (0923 26422).

COUNTRY PARKS, COMMONS AND WOODLANDS

See also Knebworth House in Gardens and in Heritage: Historic Houses.

Aldenham Country Park
(01 953 9602) P (fee)
This is a perfect setting for a day out. A children's corner with small farm animals, cattle in the meadows, picnic areas, adventure playground, miles of quiet walks, a 65-acre lake, fishing and boating. Guided walks, craft shows, exhibitions, family entertainments (contact park manager for details). Helpers welcomed to improve wildlife habitat (ask rangers for further information).
Daily: May–August, 9–8; September–April, 9–dusk.

Ashridge Estate
The Ashridge Estate covers 6 square miles of some of the most beautiful countryside in the Chiltern Hills and includes: Aldbury Woods, Ivinghoe Beacon, Northchurch Common, Berkhamsted Common, Berkhamsted Golf Course (see Sport: Golf), Bridgewater Monument (see Heritage: Other Historic Buildings), Ashridge House (see Gardens and Heritage: Historic Houses). P
Ivinghoe Beacon can be reached from the B489 (car-park at Steps Hill). There are fine views across the Vale of Aylesbury from 700 feet above sea-level. Whipsnade Zoo is nearby (See Animals and Birds). Most of Ashridge Estate is level, and there are many fine walks through the woods and open commons. The Bridgewater Monument is the starting-point of a nature trail about 1½ miles long (see Countryside: Walks). A guide can be obtained at the shop next to the monument. Refreshments available some summer weekends. D
Monument, shop and information centre: April–end October, Monday–Thursday, 2–5; Saturday, Sunday and BHMs, 2–5.30.

Broxbourne: Bencroft Wood

3 miles W of Broxbourne. P

Bencroft Wood is shown on the 1766 map of Hertfordshire, and research by the Ranger Service suggests that it may date back hundreds of years before that. The wood was probably already planted with hornbeams at the time the map was made. (Hornbeam is a very hard wood and was used to make the handles of domestic and agricultural tools.) The wood is a pleasant place in which to take a walk, and footpaths radiate from the 2 car-parking areas. There are various glades and clearings and views over farmland to the S. A bridleway has been made for horse-riders.

Broxbourne: Lee Valley Regional Park

The Lee Valley Regional Park was created in 1967 and stretches for 23 miles from London's East End to Ware in Hertfordshire. Many of the park's amenities fall in the Broxbourne area. They include the boating centre, where you can hire rowing and motor boats, and the Lido, with its wave machine, sauna and solarium, and fountains. In Broxbourne Meadows are chalets for use at holiday times, and there are picnic sites and country walks. There is a caravan park at Dobbs Weir with spaces for 100 static and 100 towing caravans. There are many other leisure and sports amenities within the park (see Countryside: Boating; Sport etc).

Broxbourne Wood

The wood comprises a number of separate areas. Access to Broxbourne Wood proper is from Pembridge Lane, Brickendon; the Wormley Wood area from White Stubbs Lane; and Hoddesdon Park Wood from Lord Street, Hoddesdon.

The wood extends over 82 acres and is part of a large, attractive area within 16 miles of Central London. It was once part of the Broxbournebury Estate, and when this was broken up, the new owners felled the old oak and hornbeam woodland and replanted it with conifers. A large fire swept through part of the wood in 1974, and after replanting a large number of the saplings died because of the very dry spring.

Chipperfield: Chipperfield Common and Commonwood Common

Under the care of Dacorum Council, this open space of over 100 acres includes some lovely unspoilt woodland and surrounds a delightful cricket ground. On the common are some huge old Spanish chestnut trees which are said to have been planted for Isabel of Castile, the first Duchess of York, who lived and died in Kings Langley in the late 14th century.

Chorleywood Common

200 acres of common land include a 9-hole golf course (see Sport: Golf) and a riding track. There are several paths and forest glades through the woods of oak, beech and silver birch trees, as well as wide-open spaces for games and kite-flying, and a pond in one corner. There are muntjac deer in the woods, but you won't see them in daylight hours – they are very shy.

Croxley Green: Croxley Hall Woods

Access from All Saints Lane.

This mature woodland borders the Grand Union Canal and the Common Moor which was once common grazing land. Beyond it is Croxley Hall Farm, once the manor house, and nearby is the medieval tithe barn (see Heritage: Other Historic Buildings). Pleasant lanes go through the woods.

Harpenden: Harpenden Common

This expanse of 238 acres of common land stretches from the shopping centre to a mile away up the hill, rising to a height of 400 feet above sea-level. The rights of the public to enjoy the air and exercise are jealously protected, and sporting activities including golf, football and cricket are allowed only in defined areas. The annual Statty Fair is held on that part of the common nearest the town.

The other part of the common, called West Common, is on the other side of the main road to St Albans. Many attractive houses border this area.

Hatfield: Hatfield House Parkland

This is 1,500 acres surrounding Hatfield House (see Heritage: Historic Houses). P

The first parkland here was enclosed by the monks of Ely in the 13th century. There are also formal gardens (see Gardens) and an arbour of lime trees surrounding beds of old English flowers and a fountain. Dogs not admitted.

Daily: 10.30–8.

Hatfield: Symonds Hyde Great Wood

N of the road from Stanborough to St Albans. Entrance is from Hammonds Lane.

This is an area of old oak and hornbeam coppice, with young birch and open grass and heathland. There is plenty of wildlife in the various habitats.

Hemel Hempstead: Gadebridge Park

Bordering the old town of Hemel Hempstead.

Excavations revealed a settlement here in pre-Roman times, and the remains of a Roman villa were found in the park. The villa was built in AD 350 and housed the largest bath known in Britain. Today nothing is visible on the site. The 300-acre park runs alongside the River Gade. There is plenty of play equipment for children, swings, slides, climbing-frames and roundabout. There is also putting and a pool. The Gade Valley Nature Trail starts in the park.

Daily.

Letchworth: Norton Common

Next to the ancient highway of Icknield Way.

In 63 acres of unspoilt grass and woodland are a playground, with swings and slides, an open-air swimming-pool, tennis courts, putting green and plenty of open space for ball games letting off steam.

Northaw: Northaw Great Wood

5 miles from Hatfield on the B157 to Cuffley.

This country park covers approximately 300 acres and is a remnant of the wood that once covered the whole of Hertfordshire. The routes of several footpaths are clearly marked. Muntjac deer can sometimes be seen, and badgers, foxes and grey squirrels are among the other creatures that can be observed. 70 species of wild birds have been sighted. A folder about the wildlife can be obtained at the site. Nature trail, picnic sites and toilets.

Oxhey Woods

Bordering Pinner Hill. P

This mature woodland covering 220 acres has been established for 250 years and is now managed by the council under a Forestry Commission Broad-Leaved Grant scheme. This enables some of the mature trees to be felled for timber and new ones to be established. Many thickets of rhododendron, blackthorn and silver birch have been thinned and cleared to allow broad-leaved trees to be planted. Footpaths lead through the woods. Picnic tables.

Rickmansworth: Aquadrome

On the A404, entrance in Harefield Road. P

The Aquadrome consists of 100 acres of land and water and is part of a series of disused, filled-in gravel pits stretching from Croxley Hall Wood to Denham. They run parallel to the Grand Union Canal and in the valley of the River Colne. Footpaths have been made near the lakes, with seats and picnic tables. Watercress-growing was a local industry, and the old watercress beds are being used to create habitats for wildlife – dragonflies, amphibians and fish, besides supporting aquatic plants and creatures. Refreshments available summer weekends. Children's playground. D

Daily: April–August, 8–8; September–March, 8–sunset.
Chess Sailing Club: 0442 215916
Water-Skiing Club: 0923 777418
Windsurfing Club: 0923 771120

Rickmansworth: Bishop's Wood

Access from Shrubs Road. P

This consists of 120 acres of mainly forestry plantations but there is a country park within its boundaries. The site is a valuable ecological area which contains many species of flora and fauna. There are woodland walks radiating from a small car-park and picnic area, and visitors can see where timber is being grown and where nature conservation projects are under way. A public footpath leads through the grounds of Mount Vernon Hospital and follows the old county boundary to Oxhey Woods.

St Albans: Herts and Middx Trust for Nature Conservation

Grebe House, St Michael's, St Albans (0727 58901)

In a restored 16th-century timber-framed building, the Trust puts on displays and provides information on local wildlife in a wildlife garden. A nature trail runs through the site. Shop.

Daily: March–December, 10–4.30; Sunday, 2–4.30.

Stevenage: Fairlands Valley Park

Six Hills Way (0438 353241) P

In a valley in the centre of the town.

This park covers 120 acres and was opened in 1972. It includes an 11-acre lake which is used for sailing throughout the year. There is a children's boating-lake with a play area and three mini-paddling-pools. N of the

boating-lake is a wildlife and nature reserve. The main lake is well stocked for fishermen. The local authority sponsor sailing courses in the summer. There is a Continental-type 'trim track' for joggers in an adjoining woodland area. A section of the town's pony-riding route goes through the park. Ducks are established on the wildfowl reserve. The S end of the valley is maintained as open space and is used as a showground for fairs, gymkhanas, circuses and similar events. A concert area provides a variety of music on Sunday afternoons. Cafeteria. D
Daily.

Tewin: Hopkyns Wood
This wild corner of Tewin Wood is a nature reserve. Welwyn Natural History Society monitor the plants and ecology in the marshy meadow by the River Tewinbury.

Waltham Cross: Cedars Park Trail
Theobald's Lane, Waltham Cross
Cedars Park is the site of the medieval manor of Theobalds which was bought in 1563 by William Cecil, Lord Burghley, Secretary to Queen Elizabeth I. He built a huge house with several large courtyards on the Cedars Park site, and the Queen is known to have stayed there at least 15 times. (She stayed in many of the stately homes in England. It was cheaper than living at home!) The old Palace House which incorporated pieces of the original building was burned down in 1968, and the grounds now form part of Cedar's Park. It is a beautiful location for country walks. Pet's corner.
Daily: 9–4.30.

Watford: Cassiobury Park
Near the town centre. Access from many points on the edge of the park: Parkside Drive, Cassiobury Park Avenue, Gade Avenue and Langley Way. It can also be

reached by walking up the towpath of the Grand Union Canal.

When the Grand Union Canal was built at the end of the 18th century to link London and the Midlands, it was planned to cut through the Hertfordshire estate of the earl of Essex at Cassiobury. He demanded a large fee and insisted on the construction of a splendid bridge over the water, which can still be seen by Grove Mill. Cassiobury Park now belongs to the Borough of Watford.

The park covers 237 acres of open spaces, recreational facilities, fine trees, picnic areas, river, canal and waterfalls. It is bordered on the W by the canal and the River Gade. A nature trail has been made along the river banks and through the wooded areas. The river meanders and is an ideal spot for fishing, paddling and picnicking. You can watch long boats going through the canal lock, or take a ride on the miniature railway. There is a paddling-pool for children, and the children's apparatus is fenced off for safety. There are many different sporting facilities, including football, cricket, bowls, croquet and putting, and hard tennis courts are available. Many of the town's events take place here each year. On May Day Morris Men 'greet the dawn' just as day breaks. The 'Marafun and Carnival' take place here on the late May Bank Holiday, and the Community Fun Day in September. Refreshments in summer.

For further information contact: Amenities and Recreation Department, 15 Hempstead Road, Watford (0923 226400, ext. 2501).

Daily.

Watford: Whippendell Woods

Access from Rousebarn Lane or Grove Mill Lane. P

These woods cover 162 acres within walking distance of the town centre. Bluebells cover the ground in the spring, and there is a wide variety of flowers, mosses and fungi. There are many magnificent trees – oak, beech, larch,

Scots pine and plenty of silver birch. There are wide grassy walks and several open spaces with picnic tables and seats made from the trunks of trees that have been felled or have blown down. There are bridleways for horse-riders, and a nature trail (see Countryside: Walks). Some of the lime trees were blown down in the gales of 1987 but are to be replaced.

Nature trail and orienteering map available, and book on the flora and fauna of Whippendell Woods. Apply to: Amenities and Recreation Department, Town Hall, Watford (0923 226400, ext. 2501).
Daily.

Welwyn Garden City: Mardley Heath
N of Welwyn.
Mardley Heath covers some 90 acres of woodland in an area of natural open space for walkers and horse-riders. The heath is owned by Welwyn & Hatfield District Council, who have decreed that the area shall remain in use for the enjoyment and recreation of local residents. Muntjac deer are among the wildlife that can be seen, but they are very shy and lie still during the day, emerging to feed only at night or in the early morning.

Welwyn Garden City: Sherrardspark Wood
This part of Welwyn Garden City's Green Belt consists of sessile oak and hornbeam, typical of woodland in this part of Hertfordshire. Woodland has 6 layers: the geological strata; the soil with its mixture of bacteria, insects, worms and small mammals; the surface layer of vegetable debris, mosses and minute plants; bracken, brambles, ferns and flowering plants; above them bushes and saplings, and high above all the canopy of mature trees. Above the first layer everything is struggling for light and moisture, for growth and survival.

The wood is owned and maintained by the district council and is looked upon by the local people as an amenity above price. It is used frequently by residents and visitors, often with their dogs, and also used by horse-riders. There is plenty of opportunity for research, as little work has been done or published on the natural history of the wood or no catalogue made of its flora and fauna. Welwyn Natural History Society publishes a guide to the nature trail which runs through the wood (see Countryside: Walks).

Welwyn Garden City: Stanborough Park

Lakes: 0707 27655. Pool: 0707 22833

Between Welwyn Garden City and Hatfield.

This park is the main summer recreational park for a wide area. P

Opened in 1970, it covers 126 acres, with a park where there is a continuing programme of tree- and shrub-planting. It is popular in both winter and summer with ramblers, and bridleways have been made for horse-riders. Sailing and boating-lakes, model boating and children's lake, nature conservancy area, windsurfing, angling, sailing dinghies for hire, launching facilities for private dinghies, showers and changing accommodation, open-air pool, main and learners' pool (solar-heated), children's paddling-pool with a sandy beach, model boating-lake, Children's play area (with concrete surface and including igloo frame, swings, slides etc), 9-station trim trail round a 2-mile circuit.

Daily.

Wheathampstead: Nomansland Nature Trail

Nomansland Common lies on the W side of B651 between Wheathampstead and Sandridge. P

This land was once the boundary between land held by the Abbey of St Albans and Westminster Abbey – hence its name. The boundary of the parishes of Sandridge and Wheathampstead still goes across it. The Herts & Middx Trust for Nature Conservation designed the nature trail, which starts in the lane opposite the Wicked Lady public house. This whole area is associated with the legendary 17th-century highwaywoman 'wicked Lady Ferrers'; hence the name of the pub.

A well-defined route goes past South End Cottages, then W for ½ mile to the junction with Ferrers Lane. There is then a sharp left turn and the path skirts the gravel pit back to South End Cottages. The common was once used for grazing but is now given over totally to recreation. There is a published guide to the flora and fauna available from the trust, from whom further information can be obtained: Herts & Middx Trust for Nature Conservation Ltd, Grebe House, St Michaels Street, St Albans (0727 58901).

NATURE RESERVES

There are 3 defined nature reserves in the county: Stocker's Lake, Rickmansworth, adjoining the Batchworth Lake Aquadrome; Rye House Marsh Reserve, Hoddesdon, and Tring Reservoirs. The first of these is administered by the Herts & Middx Trust for Nature Conservation (Offley Place, Offley, Hitchin), from whom permits may be obtained for access to the lakes for birdwatching etc; the second is administered by the Royal Society for the Protection of Birds; and the third by the Nature Conservancy Council – i.e., it is a national nature reserve. However, there are countless other locations where birds and other wildlife abound. The main such locations are the country parks and common lands described elsewhere in this chapter.

Rickmansworth: Stocker's Lake

Stocker's Lake is administered by the Herts & Middx Trust for Nature Conservation, and it is necessary to get a permit from them for access to the lake and its surrounding land. Among the birds to be seen there are great crested grebe, mallard, mute swans, bewick swans, greylag and Canada geese, tufted duck, pochards and heron. Winter visitors include redshank, oyster catchers, dunlin and cormorants. Water vole, water rats, toads and frogs abound, as well as hedgehogs, badgers, squirrels, stoats and foxes. Butterflies, dragonfly and damsel flies also thrive, as do many plants which are to be found only in protected wetlands.

Stanstead Abbots: Rye House Marsh Reserve (RSPB)
Rye Road, Hoddesdon (0992 460031)
This reserve which is next to the car-park at Rye House (see Heritage: Historic Houses), provides an opportunity to observe the birds which inhabit marshes and wetlands. Weekends, 9–3.

Tring: Tring Reservoirs National Nature Reserve (NCC)
1 mile N of Tring. Parking opposite the Angler's Retreat on the B489.
These reservoirs were built in 1802-39 to store water for the Grand Junction Canal, now the Grand Union Canal, which reaches its summit of 400 feet nearby. The arm of the canal to Wendover was dug to supply water to replace that used by the locks, and then 4 reservoirs were built on marshy land. These reservoirs now form a nature reserve, and a nature trail which starts at the Angler's Retreat is nearly 2 miles long but can be shortened to 1 mile if wished. Trees and marshland flora can be studied here, but the main interest is the abundance of the birdlife. Hides are provided for the use of birdwatchers. Large flocks of ducks winter here, and thousands of gulls. Migratory waders visit the mudflats, and herons are attracted by the plentiful fish supply. One of the most attractive birds that can be seen is the great crested grebe, which carries its young on its back as it swims in the water.

PICNIC SITES

Here are some of the places where tables and seats have been provided so that you can have a picnic. Some of them are in places where you may have to pay an entry fee. You can always find your own spot to have a picnic, but do not trespass on private property and follow the Country Code at all times.

See the Countryside section for the following: Aldenham Country Park, Aldenham; Ashridge Estate, Ashridge; Aquadrome, Rickmansworth; Bishops Wood, Rickmansworth; Broxbourne Lee Valley Regional Park; Cassiobury Park, Watford; Chorleywood Common, Chorleywood; Gadebridge Park, Hemel Hempstead; Knebworth Park, Knebworth; Letchworth Norton Common; Northaw Great Wood, Northaw; Oxhey Woods, South Oxhey; Fairlands Valley Park, Stevenage, and Whippendell Woods, Watford.

For Benington Lordship Gardens, Stevenage, see Gardens, and for Cherry Trees Farm, Belsize, near Sarratt; Wimpole Hall Park and Home Farm; and Woodside Farm and Wildlife Park, Aley Green, see Farms.

TOURS

TOURS BY CAR

Armed with a good map of the county – (e.g. Bartholomew's *Herts and Bucks Leisure Map*), most people will wish to decide for themselves which routes to take and which places to visit *en route*. However, a few suggested tours covering some of the villages described in the book are listed here.

AROUND RICKMANSWORTH

(APPROX. 30 MILES)	**PLACES TO VISIT**
The Chalfonts:	*Chiltern Open Air Museum* (see Heritage: Museums)
Chenies:	*Chenies Manor* (see Heritage: Historic Houses); summer only, Wednesday and Thursday, p.m.)
Latimer:	*Sarratt* village green (see Towns and Villages: Villages).
Flaunden:	*Aquadrome* at Rickmansworth (see Countryside: Country Parks)
Bovingdon	
Sarratt	
Rickmansworth	
Chorleywood	

AROUND ST ALBANS

(APPROX. 40 MILES)	**PLACES TO VISIT**
Harpenden:	Ashridge Estate (see Countryside: Country Parks) and the Bridgewater Monument (see Heritage: Other Historic Buildings)
Redbourn	
Flamstead:	The stocks and pond at Aldbury village (see Towns and Villages: Villages)
Great Gaddesden:	Parish church of St Mary at Hemel Hempstead (see Heritage: Churches)
Ashridge	
Aldbury	
Hemel Hempstead	
Abbots Langley	
Harpenden	

AROUND STEVENAGE

(APPROX. 54 MILES)	**PLACES TO VISIT**
Stevenage:	*Royston Cave* (see Heritage: Archaeological Sites)

Walkern:	*Royston Priory Gardens* (see Gardens: Town Parks)
Clothall:	*Ashwell Church and Museum* (see Heritage: Churches, and Museums)
Kelshall:	*Benington Lordship Gardens* (see Gardens)
Royston	
Ashwell	
Buntingford:	St Peter's Church, Buntingford
Cottered	
The Mundens	
Benington	
Shephall	
Stevenage:	Church of St Andrew and St George, Stevenage:

AROUND WARE (APPROX. 40 MILES)	**PLACES TO VISIT**
Ware	*Scott's Grotto* (see Heritage: Other Historic Buildings)
Puckeridge and Standon	*The Gazebos* along the River Lee (see Heritage: Other Historic Buildings)
Braughing	*St Andrew's Church* at *Much Hadham* and the village (see Heritage: Churches and Towns and Villages: Villages)
Barkway	
Barley:	Village cage and St Margaret's Church
	Anstey
	The Pelhams
	Much Hadham
	Widford
	Ware

AROUND WELWYN	**PLACES TO VISIT**
Welwyn	Old Knebworth and *Knebworth House* (see Heritage: Historic Houses). St Mary's Church, Old Knebworth

Knebworth
Hitchin
Pirton
Lilley
The Waldens
Wheathampstead
Ayot St Lawrence
Ayot St Peter
Welwyn

Hitchin parish church of St Mary (see Heritage: Churches)

Shaw's Corner at Ayot St Lawrence (see Heritage: Historic Houses)

A Literary Tour of Hertfordshire

Several well-known authors have had close connections with the county, and this car tour, which covers a round trip of 40 miles, takes in some of the places associated with them.

ST ALBANS: FRANCIS BACON (1561-1626)

This essayist, philosopher and statesman was made Lord Chancellor in 1618 and was raised to the peerage, taking the title of Lord Verulam. Gorhambury was Bacon's estate. He is buried in St Michael's Church, and there is a monument to him in the chancel. Gorhambury House is open to the public. (See Heritage: Historic Houses.)

AYOT ST LAWRENCE: GEORGE BERNARD SHAW (1856-1950)

The Irish dramatist, music critic and essayist lived from 1906 until his death at Shaw's Corner in Ayot St Lawrence. Owned and administered by the National Trust, Shaw's Corner remains as it was in his lifetime, with his hats still hanging in the hall, and his pens, dictionary and typewriter still on his desk. (See Heritage: Historic Houses.)

KNEBWORTH HOUSE: CHARLES DICKENS (1812-70)

Dickens was a lifelong friend of Sir Bulwer Lytton, who owned Knebworth House, and was a frequent visitor. He led a star-studded group of actors in a performance of Ben Jonson's *Every Man in His Humour* there. The correspondence between Dickens and Sir Bulwer Lytton can be seen at Knebworth. (See Heritage: Historic Houses.)

WESTMILL: CHARLES LAMB (1775-1834)

Lamb was the first great author to write for children, and with his sister Mary wrote *Tales from Shakespeare*. In 1812 he inherited Button Snap, a thatched cottage in Westmill but sold it 3 years later. The cottage is not open to the public.

TOURS BY CYCLE

Cyclists can adapt to their own use the suggestions made for motorists. Again, *Bartholomew's Herts and Bucks Leisure Map* (scale 1.6 miles to 1 inch) would be a useful guide, but cyclists may prefer to use the Ordnance Survey Landranger series (scale 1¼ inches to 1 mile). Sheet 166 covers most of the county.

A booklet, *Cycling in Hertfordshire*, published by the Cyclists Touring Club and the Sports Council (20 pages, price 30p) is available from tourist information centres. It sets out 8 routes in various parts of the county as follows:

St Albans to the Ayots (and back)	18 miles
St Albans to Epping Green (and back)	24 miles
Hemel Hempstead to Aldbury (and back)	22 miles
Hertford to Barwick (and back)	20 miles
Bishop's Stortford to the Hadhams (and back)	20 miles
Bishop's Stortford to Westmill (and back)	20 miles
Stevenage to Woodend (and back)	18 miles
Stevenage to Ashwell (and back)	20 miles

WALKS

Much of the enjoyment of walking comes from going where fancy leads and not being constrained to follow set routes. Of course, one must observe rights of way and follow the Country Code, but within those limits the walker has the freedom of hundreds of miles of ancient ways traversing the length and breadth of the county. To enjoy that freedom, it is sensible to use the relevant sheets of the Ordnance Survey Pathfinder series (scale 1:25000, i.e. about 2½ inches to 1 mile), which includes all rights of way. With these maps, you can work out your own routes, picking up points of interest mentioned elsewhere in this book.

Set out below are brief outlines of officially designated walks, byways, bridleways, town trails, country walks and waterside walks. As regards waterside walks, it is probably worth making the point that very few canal towpaths are public rights of way, but the British Waterways Board allows free access to these paths throughout the country.

BYWAYS AND BRIDLEWAYS

Benington (4½ miles)

This is a fairly short route in gently rolling countryside E of Benington and passes through mainly arable farmland.

Ardeley–Wood End (6½ miles)

This circuit includes 2 stretches on roads but mostly uses bridleways. It goes across mostly arable farmland with some fields of sheep.

Clothall–Wallington (10 miles)

You should take this route anti-clockwise so as to avoid constantly crossing roads when making right-hand turns. Most of it, however, goes through open landscape and ploughed fields. There are some good views of Cambridgeshire in the N section.

GUIDED WALKS

In 1988 the Herts/Barnet Countryside Management Service produced a programme of guided walks in the Hertfordshire countryside, starting off with an International Dawn Chorus Day, with meeting-places at a variety of country parks at 4 a.m. to hear the Dawn Chorus! These guided walks discover attractive villages, old lanes, tracks, ancient woodland, lost villages, historic buildings, churches etc. Most have a theme. They are taken at a leisurely pace and are suitable for the whole family. They vary in length from 2 to 12 miles, and they are all circular, returning to the starting-point. For further information ring 0992 555250.

TOWN TRAILS AND COUNTRY WALKS

Amwell Walkway

Near Stanstead Abbots. Interesting wildlife and flowers and of particular interest to birdwatchers. Starting just N of Stanstead Abbots on the Holycross Road, this walk follows the former Buntingford Branch Railway.

Ashridge Park

There is a marked nature trail through this National Trust woodland. (See Countryside: Country Parks.) A leaflet is available from the trust's office at the Bridgewater Monument.

Ayot Greenway

This walk follows the track bed of the now disused railway from Luton and Dunstable to Welwyn Junction, which was opened in 1860. By the middle of 1971 all the track had been lifted, and for 7 years it lay undisturbed. Now the Herts/Barnet Countryside Management Service carry out a programme of maintenance of the track, making it a quiet route for walkers and horse-riders whilst protecting the wildlife that abounds on the embankments and cuttings.

A leaflet is available from the County Planning and Estates Officer, County Hall, Hertford (0992 555265).

Bishop's Stortford

This is a route through the medieval town centre. Leaflets entitled *Town Trail* and *A Walk About* are published by the Local History Society. Telephone the information office at 2 The Causeway, Bishop's Stortford (0279 55261).

Lee Valley Leisure Park

(0992 717711)

There are plenty of walks in this park, which extends 23 miles along the River Lee from Ware to London. (See Countryside: Country Parks.)

Broxbourne Woods

There are footpaths, bridleways and picnic areas in these woods. (See Countryside: Country Parks.)

Hertford: Cole Green Way

This route follows the course of the track of the now disused Hertford, Luton & Dunstable Railway. You can go from the Hertford Viaduct as far as the A414 at Cole Green. Cycling, horse-riding and walking are all permissible.

Letchworth

Letchworth Garden City Corporation have opened a number of attractive walks which have been established and maintained by various local groups. None is more than 4½ miles long, and the shortest is 1 mile.

Route 1 starts at the Fox Inn at Willian and passes under the A1(M) before returning to base.

Route 2 also starts at the Fox Inn, Willian, and goes near Great Wymondley before going back to base.

Route 3 starts at the Pond at Willian and includes part of the Wymondley road.

Route 4 follows the route of the Great North Road.
Route 5 covers part of Nortonbury.
Route 6 starts at the Three Horseshoes public house.
It crosses the Stotfold road and goes parallel with the River Ivel before returning to Nortron.

The leaflet describing these walks in greater detail is available from the Information Centre, Hitchin Library, Paynes Park (0462 34738).

Northaw Great Wood

3 paths of varying lengths are marked through the woodland. (See Countryside: Country Parks.)

Stevenage: Monks Wood Nature Trail

There are 2 paths through Monks and Whomerley Woods. You should wear stout shoes for both. Both are waymarked and both start and finish at Fairlands Valley car-park. Much of the work in maintaining the woods and the paths is undertaken by volunteers. If you are interested in helping, there is a regular programme of work. Please contact the Ranger at Stevenage Lodge, Frobisher Drive, Stevenage (0438 725416).

Ware Priory Gardens

There is a Fisherman's Walk along the River Lee.

Ware

A town walk and riverside walks. Leaflets are available from Ware Library (0920 2683).

Watford: Whippendell Woods

Footpaths are marked through these 200 acres of woodland. One of them leads through the West Herts Golf Course and leads to the canal and Cassiobury Park, through which there are many footpaths. A nature trail has been produced to take you through the woods, and an orienteering map is also available. These can be obtained from the Amenities and Recreation Department, Town Hall, Watford (0923 226400).

Welwyn Garden City: Sherrardspark Wood

A woodland nature trail is marked out through the woods. It takes about 2 hours to complete. A leaflet and map describing the trail are available from the information centre at Campus West (0707 332880).

Welwyn Garden City Town Trail

A leaflet describing the route of the town trail has been produced by the curator of the Welwyn Hatfield Museum Service. It is available from The Old Mill House Museum, Mill Green, Hatfield (07072 71362).

WATERSIDE WALKS

Hertford

The E Herts District Council has produced a leaflet entitled *Hertford's Waterside Walks*, and this is available from the information centre at The Castle in Hertford (0279 55261). The 3 routes described in detail are

River Lee: Town centre to Hertford Lock (2 miles)

River Lee: Town centre to Ware (3¼ miles)

River Beane: Hertford to Waterford to Stapleford to Watton-at-Stone (4½ miles)

St Albans

The Countryside Commission have produced a leaflet entitled *The Ver-Colne Valley Walk*. It is available from the information centre at 37 Chequer Street, St Albans (0727 64511). The route starts at Redbourn and roughly follows the River Ver through St Albans to Park Street, and the River Colne to Bricket Wood, and Garston to Watford. It is about 15 miles long. The leaflet includes a British Rail timetable for the return journey!

Eating and Drinking

No attempt has been made in this book to give a comprehensive list of places of refreshment – whether cafés, coffee-shops, pubs or restaurants. That must be left to specialist guidebooks on good food and drink. However, reference is made to facilities provided on the spot by some of the places described in other chapters, and a fairly brief selection has been made of other establishments which are either close to the places visited or, in the opinion of the author, worth visiting on their own account for one reason or another. Inclusion is not intended to imply special commendation, nor does omission imply any condemnation. To put the matter in perspective, it is worth pointing out that there are over 800 pubs in Hertfordshire, and the number of cafés, tea-rooms and restaurants is, of course, much bigger than that.

In the space available, it is not possible to go into detail about the range of food and drink provided, and in any case things change so quickly in this field that there is a high risk of being seriously out of date. In general, the pub entries have been confined to those which offer food during their normal opening hours. The short list of restaurants has been drawn up on the basis that eating out is the main purpose of the expedition rather than incidental to some other activity. Exceptions to this principle are the lists of Little Chef and Happy Eater restaurants, which are shown because they are known quantities conveniently situated by the side of main roads.

INNS

Abbreviations used in this section are as follows:

BF = Bar food
FR = Family room
G = Games
P = Parking. Most inns have limited parking space; P indicates that there is a reasonable area for parking.
R = Restaurant

Aldbury

GREYHOUND: In centre of the village, by the duck pond, this pub is now offering a wide choice of food at reasonable prices. BF

VALIANT TROOPER: In Trooper Lane in the direction of Aldbury Common. Some tables in the small, pretty garden at the rear. BF/R

Amwell

Amwell is on a minor road SW of Wheathampstead.

ELEPHANT & CASTLE: Seats outside under the trees. BF/R

Ashwell

BUSHEL & STRIKE: BF/R

ROSE & CROWN: 60 High Street, Ashwell. BF/R

THREE TUNS: Yet another attractive pub in this N Hertfordshire village. BF

Ayot St Lawrence

BROCKET ARMS: Located close to the ruined church (see Heritage: Churches), this comfortable pub's catering includes a traditional Sunday roast lunch. Tables on the lawn at the back of the house. BF/R

Baldock

THE WHITE LION: 46 High Street. BF

Barkway

CHAISE & PAIR: A small modernized pub. BF/R

Barley

FOX & HOUNDS: The pub brews its own beer. Picnic tables on the grass bordering the car-park. BF/G/P

Belsize

THE PLOUGH: At the junction of Dunny Lane, Flaunden Lane and Poles Hill in the hamlet of Belsize, this cosy pub is a useful place for refreshment, serving very reasonably priced food (but not on Saturday or Sunday evenings). Small garden. BF

Berkhamsted

THE SWAN: 135 High Street. This is a popular town-centre pub dating from the 17th century, with 2 connecting bars offering good fare and friendly service. BF/P

Bovingdon

HALFWAY HOUSE: Hempstead Road. BF

Boxmoor

THE FISHERY: As the name suggests, this pub is by the side of the Grand Union Canal (and the River Bulbourne), and it has a lovely view of passing boats; also waterside tables. Decent food, good service. BF

THREE BLACKBIRDS: 194 St John's Road. With the Dacorum Sports Centre and cricket field nearby, this is a conveniently located pub offering good-value bar food. BF

Bushey

HORSE & CHAINS: 79 High Street. Good bar food Monday–Saturday, with set lunches and grills. Garden. BF/P

ROYAL OAK: 42 Sparrows Herne. A pub which serves some rare brews. BF

Chenies

RED LION: Chenies is just in Buckinghamshire, but this pub is included because it is convenient for anyone visiting Chenies Manor (see Heritage: Historic Houses). It offers good fare. BF/P

Cheshunt

VICTORIA: 147 Turners Hill. Fairly close to the town centre, council offices etc, the Victoria provides decent pub food lunchtime and evening.

Chipperfield

TWO BREWERS: Enviably situated by the village green and cricket field, this is a comfortable old inn. BF/R/P

Chorleywood

GARDEN GATE: Rickmansworth Road. Very handy for the common and cricket field. BF/R/P

WHITE HORSE: Rickmansworth Road. Almost as handy for the common and cricket field as the Garden Gate, but on the opposite side of the road. Good pub food. P

THE SPORTSMAN: Station Approach. BF/R/P

Colney Heath

CROOKED BILLETT: On the B6426 which runs through the village, this pub offers not only a wide range of beers etc but also cold milk and milk cocktails. Garden, with pets' corner – pony rides in summer. BF/FR

Croxley Green

THE ARTICHOKE: Right on the green, this pub has open fires, gas lighting, a parrot – and a good standard of food. BF/P

TWO BRIDGES: Very handy for the Watford Marina by the canal bridge, this pub is just off the roundabout which forms the junction of Watford Road, Baldwins Lane and Rickmansworth Road, Watford. Excellently appointed, comfortable and offering a good choice of food at the counter. BF/P

Dane End

From the A602 at Watton-at-Stone, take a minor road through Whempstead to Dane End.

THE PLOUGH: The pub is notable for having a full-size theatre organ in its specially built lounge extension, accompaniment to meals on Friday–Sunday evenings and some Sunday lunchtimes. Garden, leading to fields beyond. BF

Flaunden

GREEN DRAGON: A warmly welcoming pub which will take orders for bar food by phone, so that they are ready when you arrive. Lawn to the side with tables. Canaries and budgies make a cheerful sight and sound. BF/R/P

Frithsden

ALFORD ARMS: This pub, which brews its own beers, is one of a number of pubs handily placed for a visit for the Ashridge Estate (see Countryside: Country Parks) and also for the vineyard at Frithsden (see Farms). BF/R

Great Offley

GREEN MAN: Conveniently placed if you are visiting the Icknield Way (see Heritage: Archaeological Sites). Terrace at the back with tables; extensive views. BF/R

Halls Green

Halls Green is on a minor road leading from the B1037 at Cromer to Weston and Letchworth.

THE RISING SUN: This pub is useful is you are visiting the Cromer windmill (see Heritage: Other Historic Buildings). It provides good home-cooked food, and there is a large garden. BF/G

Harpenden

THE FOX: 469 Luton Road. Impressive range of meals served in the saloon; comfortable lounge. BF

HARPENDEN ARMS: 188 High Street. BF

OLD COCK INN: High Street. Comfortable town pub. BF

THREE HORSESHOES: East Common. If you are looking for lunch in this area (not on Sundays), this old, white-painted pub has much to recommend it: good food; peaceful location; walks over the common to work up an appetite. BF

Hemel Hempstead

OLDE KING'S ARMS: 41 High Street. In the old part of town, this pub is close to the Old Town Hall and Gadebridge Park (see Arts and Countryside: Town Parks respectively). BF

MARCHMONT ARMS: At Piccotts End, this pub serves bar food at lunchtimes, Monday–Saturday, and a carvery and restaurant are in operation Tuesday–Saturday evenings. BF/R

Hertford

OLD BARGE: The Folly, leading over the canal from Bull Plain in the town centre. Right by the side of the canal. BF/R/P

SALISBURY ARMS: Fore Street, town centre. This old coaching inn offers British and Chinese food. R/P

THE WOOLPACK: Mill Bridge. Another town-centre pub with a riverside setting. Wide range of hot and cold food. FR/G

Hexton

THE RAVEN: Handy for visits to see the stretch of the Icknield Way near Mortgrove or the site of Ravensburgh Castle (see Heritage: Archaeological Sites), the pub has a comfortable dining-room (no food on Sundays, though). Garden play area for children. BF/R

Hitchin

NEW FOUND OUT: 181 Stevenage Road at the S end of the town, handy for Priory Park and only a short distance into the attractive town centre. BF

SAILOR BOY: 95 Woolgrove Road, N of the town on the edge of the industrial area, this pub is fairly close to the railway station and the North Herts College. BF

RED HART: Thought to be the town's oldest building, situated in Bucklersbury in the town centre. Comfortable place but serving lunch only. BF

Ickleford

North of Hitchin on the line of the Icknield Way.

OLD GEORGE: An old pub by the churchyard. BF

King's Langley

LANGLEYS: On the A41 on the Hemel Hempstead side of King's Langley, this big pub stands well back from the road. Spacious garden and play area. BF/R/FR/P

Knebworth

Knebworth is separated from Old Knebworth (where Knebworth House is situated) by the A1(M), but the distance is not great.

STATION HOTEL: Park Lane. A useful pub in this area. BF

Lemsford

CROOKED CHIMNEY: On the B653, handily placed for Brocket Hall, this is a spruce pub. BF/R/P

Letchworth

THREE HORSESHOES: This pub, which is in Norton on the N outskirts of Letchworth, provides a good range of bar food Monday–Saturday at lunchtime, set lunches on Sunday, and grills in the restaurant in the evenings, Monday–Saturday. Garden. BF/R/P

TWO CHIMNEYS: Stotfold Road. On the W periphery of the town, this pub is fairly handy for a visit to the Standalone Children's Farm (see Farms). BF/P

Letty Green

COWPER ARMS HOTEL: Cole Green Lane, just off the A414 Welwyn Garden City to Hertford road, and a useful staging-post between the two towns, particularly if you are visiting Panshanger Aerodrome. BF/R/P

Little Gaddesden

BRIDGEWATER ARMS: Surrounded by National Trust property (Ashridge Park, Hudnall Common), this comfortable pub serves home-brewed ale. Well placed for visiting Longford Children's Farm (see Farms). BF/R/FR

London Colney

GREEN DRAGON: Waterside by the River Colne, this is a delightful, wistaria-covered old pub, with a wealth of beams and horsebrasses. It is included because of its aesthetic appeal and its proximity to Salisbury Hall (see Heritage: Museums). Good lunches are served Monday–Friday and snacks Monday–Saturday, but evening meals are not available. Outside tables. BF/R

Newgate Street

COACH & HORSES: 1 mile north of Cuffley, this pub is very handy for visits to the country park in Northaw Great Wood (see Countryside: Country Parks). It serves bar meals and snacks every day except Sunday. (Rolls available Sunday evenings.) Large wooded garden; tables on lawn. BF/FR

Preston

RED LION: A convenient place for a stop if you are visiting the Waldens or, indeed, Preston village itself to see the Bunyan Chapel or Bunyan's Dell, where Bunyan often preached. Unusually, this pub is owned by the village.

There is a paddock of goats and rabbits. BF/FR

Puckeridge

A useful staging-post on the A10 between Ware and Royston, especially if visiting Standon to view the craft cabinet- and clock-making, or Collier's End for pony trekking.

CROWN & FALCON: A very old but comfortably modernized pub. BF/R

WHITE HART: Another old-established pub. Fish a speciality. Garden and drinking-area outside. BF/R

Rickmansworth

YE OLDE GREENE MANNE: Batchworth Heath. Convenient for visit to Moor Park Mansion and golf course (see Heritage: Historic Houses and Sport: Golf) and Bishop's Wood (see Countryside: Country Parks). BF/P

FEATHERS INN: In the town centre (W side of Church Street), this 16th-century inn is an interesting refreshment point; food at lunchtime only. BF

Rushden

MOON & STARS: Off the A507 Baldock to Buntingford road, this picturesque pub is worth a little detour. Meals (except Sundays) and snacks (except Sunday lunchtime). Garden, climbing-frame and swings. BF

St Albans

BARLEY MOW: Tyttenhanger Green (off the A405 just over a mile E of the A6/A1081 roundabout). This pub is notable for its great range of real ales. It is handy if you have been visiting Aylett's nurseries (see Gardens: Garden Centres). Tables outside; swings for children. BF

FIGHTING COCKS: 16 Abbey Mill Lane, off George Street, through abbey gateway. Although you can drive to the pub, it may, depending on the time of year, be easier to park elsewhere and walk down. This almost circular pub dates back some 400 years and for its first 300 years was called the Round House. Very handy for Verulamium Park and the Roman remains (see Heritage: Archaeological Sites). Bar meals at lunchtime (not Sunday) and snacks Monday–Saturday lunchtime (also Sunday in summer). BF/FR

FLEUR DE LYS: French Row. A comfortably modernized medieval building right in the heart of the city. Park elsewhere. BF

GARIBALDI: 61 Albert Street, Just off Holywell Hill BF

ROSE & CROWN: In St Michael's Street, which may be approached either from the A414 (Bluehouse Hill) or from the city centre via George Street and Fishpool Street. Handy for Verulamium Park and the Roman town (see Heritage: Archaeological Sites). BF

THREE HORSESHOES: Hatfield Road. On the E side of St Albans, this is a useful staging-post *en route* for Welwyn, Hatfield and further destinations in E and N Hertfordshire. BF/R/P

WHITE HART: Holywell Hill. This is an historic inn dating back to the 1530s, when it was let as an inn by the abbey. It has a beamed lounge with 18th-century oak panelling, a minstrels' gallery and delightful old-world bars. BF/R/P

Sarratt

THE COCK: Handy for walkers and those visiting Sarratt's rather unusual church (see Heritage: Churches), which is just across the road (Church Lane). BF/FR/P

Sawbridgeworth

WHITE LION: London Road. A handy place for lunch if you are sampling the delights of this extreme E part of the county. No meals in the evenings. BF

Shenley

PINKS: Rectory Lane, about 1 mile from the village in the direction of the A6 and M25, this beautifully situated pub is useful if you are visiting the Mosquito Aircraft Museum at Salisbury Hall (see Heritage: Museums). Tables and chairs under awnings with view of delightful gardens. Good food. BF/P

Stevenage

THE FISHERMAN: Fishers Green, at the N end of the town and tucked away near the Lister Hospital and the A1(M). This is a useful family pub, with plenty of children's games. Barbecues on fine evenings. BF/P

THE WHITE LION: High Street, Old Town, about ½ mile from the station and near the King George V Playing Fields. BF/R/P

THE YORKSHIRE GREY: 15 High Street, Old Town. Location similar to that of the White Lion. BF/P

Tewin

PLUME OF FEATHERS: Upper Green Road. A convenient port of call if you are visiting the Tewin Mill Fish Farm (see Animals: Aquatic Life) or Hopkyns Wood (see Countryside: Country Parks). A friendly and comfortable pub. BF/R/P

Tring

COW ROAST: London Road on the E outskirts of Tring. Tables outside at the back. BF/R/P

KINGS ARMS: King Street. Only a short walk from the town centre or from the Zoological Museum (see Heritage: Museums). BF/P

Walkern

WHITE LION: A warmly welcoming small pub, useful in conjunction with a visit to Benington Lordship (see Gardens). BF/R

Ware

NEW ROSE & CROWN: 35 Watton Road. Very convenient if you are visiting the Fanshawe Swimming Pool (see Sport:

Swimming) in Park Road or walking along one of the footpaths alongside the River Lee towards Hertford (see Countryside: Walks) and feel like taking some refreshment at that point. BF/P

Wareside

On the B1004 E of Ware.

WHITE HORSE: This pub is a useful resting-point *en route* for Much Hadham and Bishop's Stortford. BF

Watton-at-Stone

Watton-at-Stone is almost exactly mid-way between Hertford and Stevenage, and so this is a very good place to take refreshment.

GEORGE & DRAGON: First-class bar food, with a wide choice, including seafood. Tables in small herb garden. BF/R/P

Welwyn

THE STEAMER: London Road. Lunches and evening meals in dining section. Tables outside. BF/P

THE WELLINGTON: High Street, Old Welwyn. Reasonably handy for the Ayot Way and Sherrard's Park nature trails (see Countryside: Walks). BF/R/P

Welwyn Garden City

LUDWICK ARMS: Hall Grove. Good provision for family visits; well-equipped play area; conservatory with games, TV. Live entertainment on many Sundays. BF

Wheathampstead

WICKED LADY: Nomansland Common (see Countryside: Country Parks). If you've worked up an appetite by taking an energetic walk on the common, this pub supplies the food to satisfy it. No bar food Sunday evening. Covered terrace in garden. BF/R/P

MAIN-ROAD STOPS

Roadside restaurants are very convenient for travellers, and the popular Little Chef and Happy Eater restaurants in Hertfordshire are listed below.

Little Chefs
Astwick, 3 miles N of Letchworth: A1 northbound.
Bourne End, 2 miles W of Hemel Hempstead: A41.
Bricket Wood, 2 miles N of Watford: A405, southbound.
Cheshunt, 6 miles S of Hoddesdon: A10 Great Cambridge Road.
Chiswell Green, between Watford and St Albans: A405 on the roundabout.
Flamstead, Watling Street, near Markyate: A5, 3 miles N of Harpenden.
Radlett, Watling Street: A5, 1½ miles N of Radlett.
Royston, Baldock Road: A505

Happy Eaters
Baldock, Great North Road: A1 Hinxworth.
Royston, Newmarket Road: A505, Heydon.
Ware, High Road: A10, High Cross.

REFRESHMENT ROOMS AT PLACES TO VISIT

For location and opening times, please consult the relevant chapter/section, viz. Farms, Gardens, Sport: Leisure Centres, Heritage: Historic Houses, etc.

Ashridge Estate
Tea kiosk next to the information centre at the Bridgewater monument. Open at weekends in the summer.

Belsize near Sarratt: Cherry Trees Farm
Wholefood tea-rooms for lunch and tea; children's parties by arrangement.

Benington Lordship Gardens
Home-made teas on Sundays and BHs.

Broxbourne: Paradise Park and Woodland Zoo
Refreshment/dining-rooms.

Chenies: Chenies Manor
Afternoon teas.

Cheshunt: Grundy Park Leisure Centre
Refreshment bar serving this multi-purpose sports complex.

Chorleywood Common: Wyatts Tea-Rooms
Just off the Rickmansworth road, at the junction with Solesbridge Lane, the tea-rooms serve morning coffee, afternoon tea and cream teas. Not open Monday and Friday.

Hatfield House: Old Palace Yard Coffee-Shop
Light meals and refreshments; pre-booked lunch and tea available for parties of 10 or more. Closed Monday (except BHs) and GF.

Hemel Hempstead: Dacorum Sports Centre
Café – for drinks and light meals.

Knebworth House: The Barns
Licensed restaurant for visitors. P

Letchworth: North Herts Leisure Centre
Cafeteria; birthday teas; lunch.

Letchworth: Standalone Farm
Café for light refreshments.

Luton Hoo
Tea-rooms and picnic area.

Markyate: High Winds Children's Farm
Tea on the lawn in summer; picnic area.

Rickmansworth: Aquadrome
Refreshments at summer weekends.

Royston: Wimpole Hall
Light lunches and teas in Great Dining-Room. Simple refreshments also available at Wimpole Home Farm.

St Albans Abbey: Chapter House Refectory
Family restaurant.

St Albans: Sally Lunn's 14th-Century Eating-House
Open Monday–Saturday evenings and for Sunday lunch, in 5 olde-worlde dining-rooms.

St Albans: The Gardens of the Rose, Chiswell Green
Licensed cafeteria.

Stevenage: Leisure Centre
Cafeteria; birthday teas.

Stevenage: Roger Harvey Garden Centre
Country kitchen open daily for coffee, hot/cold lunches, teas, Cornish cream teas.

Watford Leisure Centre
Bar and cafeteria.

Welwyn Garden City: Gosling Stadium
Lounge bar with accommodation for 244 people, open lunchtime and evening; adjoining cafeteria for light meals and snacks.

Whipsnade Zoological Park
Cafeterias.

RESTAURANTS

Baldock: Zeus (Greek)
20b High Street, Baldock (0462 893620)
Closed for lunch.

Berkhamsted: The Cook's Delight (vegetarian)
360–364 High Street, Berkhamsted (04427 3584)
Thursday–Sunday, except Sunday dinner.

Berkhamsted: La Fiorentina (Italian)
21–23 Lower King Street, Berkhamsted (04427 3003)

Chorleywood: The Peppermill
7 New Parade, Chorleywood (09278 4421)
Closed on Mondays.

Hemel Hempstead: Casanova (Italian)
75 Waterhouse Street, Hemel Hempstead (0442 47482)
Closed for lunch weekends and BHs.

Hitchin: Redcoats Farmhouse Hotel
Little Wymondley, Hitchin (0438 729500)

Old Hatfield: Salisbury
15 The Broadway, Old Hatfield (07072 62220)
Closed lunch Saturday, dinner Sunday, all day BHM.

Rickmansworth: Long Island Exchange Bar, Hotel and Restaurant
Victoria Close, Rickmansworth (0923 775211)

St Albans: Alban Tandoori (Indian)
145 Victoria Street, St Albans (0727 62111)

Welwyn: Heath Lodge Hotel Restaurant (French)
Danesbury Park Road, Welwyn (043 871 7064)
Closed lunch Saturday.

Farms

FARMS AND FARM WALKS

Belsize, Sarratt, near Rickmansworth: Cherry Trees Farm
Ollieberrie Lane, Belsize, Sarratt, Rickmansworth (09277 68289) P
Proprietors Michael and Mary Bell
See pygmy goats, guinea pigs, Jersey cows, Marans, black Orpingtons, Ardennes carthorses, Vietnamese pot-bellied pigs, Gloucester old-spot pigs, Herdwick sheep, Ryeland sheep, Soay sheep, goats, Dorset Downs, Cochins, Bantams, Hebridean sheep. See all sorts of rare breeds: pigs, piglets, sheep, lambs, horses, foals, goats, kids, cows, dogs, hens, ducks, cats, geese, rabbits and so on. Free horse and cart rides. Join in collecting the eggs. Sunday puppet theatre. Organic farm produce on sale from the farm shop; delivery service of organic farm produce – ring for details. Wholefood tea-rooms for lunch or farm teas; children's parties by arrangements; picnic facilities. Beautiful orchard playground; barbecue available for hire. Camping and caravanning (prices by arrangement).
Wednesday to Sunday, 11–late.
Admission charge (special rates for school parties).

Great Gaddesden: Longford Children's Farm
St Margarets, Great Gaddesden, Hemel Hempstead (044284 3471) P
You can spend an hour or more at this children's farm,

where many species of animals are bred and sold, including goats, peacocks, ducks, chicks, lambs, pygmy goats and their kids, rabbits and guinea pigs. Many of the animals wander around unenclosed. Playgroups, schools welcome by appointment. Farm shop sells ice-cream, drinks, home-made biscuits, honey, pet feeds, hutches, runs and pet accessories.
Daily: 9–5 Fee; under 3-year-olds free

Letchworth: Standalone Farm
Wilbury Road, Letchworth Garden City P
A Letchworth Garden City Enterprise. All enquiries to: Chief Executive, Letchworth Garden City Corporation, Estate Office, Broadway, Letchworth (0462 685211).
Signposted from all entrances to the town.
This is a working farm, raising cattle, pigs and poultry. Milk, eggs, wheat and hay are all harvested. It is a small farm of 170 acres, so only a limited number of crops can be grown at any one time. They are usually designed to provide food all the year round for the animals. Besides grass which is made into hay, there is usually some wheat and other animal-fodder crops. All the livestock is on view – cattle, sheep, pigs, poultry, turkeys, goats and a Shire horse called Warrant. In the spring there are lambs and calves, and sometimes you can see rare species of livestock. There are also an aviary, blacksmith's shop, wildfowl area (with hides to see variety of ducks, geese and waders), picnic area (indoor and outdoor), farm shop, souvenir shop, café, farm walks, farm guides. Special facilities for school parties.
One of the hides in the wildfowl area has been especially constructed for access for the disabled. D
Daily 11–5.30, including April–October BHs. Fee

Luton Markyate: Woodside Farm and Wildfowl Park
Mancroft Road, Aley Green, near Slip End, Markyate (0582 841044) P

Bring a picnic and sit and relax while the children play with their favourite pets and watch the animals and birds, which include fallow deer, pure- and rare-breed chickens and ducks, modern hybrid chicken, ornamental fowl, geese, swans, pygmy goats, Soay sheep, Jacobean and Shetland sheep, Welsh mountain black sheep, Vietnamese pigs, peacocks, peahens, rabbits, guinea pigs, chicks, ducklings and goslings. Adventure play area with swings, slides, see-saws and a tree-house. Pond. Farm shop sells fresh fruit and vegetables, fresh cow's milk, yoghurt, goat's products (milk, cheese, ice-cream), trout, fresh and frozen chicken, ducks, geese, home-made biscuits, jams, marmalades, honey and cooked meats. Free-range eggs straight from the henhouse.

Monday–Friday, 8–5.30. Saturday, 8–5.

Wildfowl Park: Monday–Saturday, from 9 a.m. Closing-time varies according to weather conditions.

Markyate: High Winds Children's Farm

Hicks Road, Markyate (0582 841198)

Just off the A5. At crossroads in Markyate turn right and then left by footbridge into Hicks Road. P

Many of the friendly animals here have been neglected or abandoned or cruelly treated. School parties are welcome, and animals can be taken to visit schools. Pony rides. Birthday parties in one of the barns by arrangement.

April–end September, Saturday, Sunday and every day during school holidays, 10–5. Weekdays by appointment.

Royston: Wimpole Hall Park and Home Farm (NT)

(0223 207801)

Just over the Hertfordshire border in Cambridgeshire, off the A603. P

Wimpole Home Farm was built in 1794 as a model farm. The great barn was designed by Sir John Soane, and in it you can see a lot of the type of farm implements and machinery that was used here over 200 years ago. Rare

breeds of animals graze in the 350 acres of parkland. Children's corner, picnic area, adventure woodland, film loft with video presentation, cart rides pulled by Suffolk Punch horses (Nelson and Gedge), Victorian stables. Watch the sheep dipping and shearing. Quiz sheet 'The Secrets of Wimpole' for children. Restaurant and tea-room at Wimpole Hall.
Level access throughout farm for the disabled. Some ramps to the animal sheds. Klaxon at farm gate to summon assistance. Braille guide. D
April–October: Tuesday–Thursday, weekends and BHMs, 10.30–5.

Stevenage: Aston Bury Farm
Aston Lane, Stevenage (0438 88302) P
Just off the A602.
This is a working dairy farm with a Friesian herd which produces 1½ million pints of milk a year. The farm is fully open to the public. You can see calves, pigs, sheep and heavy horses. (The herd is milked at 3 p.m.) Video presentation, bottling plant. School parties welcome by arrangement – staff available to answer questions.
BRING YOUR WELLINGTON BOOTS!!
March–September: Saturday, 11–5; Sunday, 12–5.

Waltham Abbey: Hayes Hill Farm
(099289 2781) P
Part of the Lee Valley Regional Park (see Countryside: Country Parks). Just off Stubbins Hall Lane, Crooked Mile. Many animals can be seen at close quarters in pens and paddocks of traditional style. Craft demonstrations on summer Sundays and BHs.

Waltham Abbey: Holyfieldhall Farm
This is a working dairy farm with 150 Friesian cattle. At 3 p.m. every day you can see them being milked in a

modern milking-parlour. Summer tractors rides sometimes available between Holyfieldhall and Hayes Hill Farms. Conducted tours. School parties welcome by arrangement.
Daily: Monday–Friday, 10–4.30; weekends and BHs, 10–6.

Waltham Cross: Capel Manor Environmental Centre and Educational Farm
Just off Bullsmoor Lane. P
At Capel Manor there is a large range of livestock, and the continuous breeding programme means that young chicks and piglets are nearly always on show. You need to book to see the milking demonstration that takes place at the end of each day. There is a varied programme for families, with events such as birdwatching for beginners, a nightwatch, map- and compass-reading and scarecrow-building.

65 acres of woodland grass and ponds; Environmental Centre and play area. Worksheets and study packs; Earth Education activities. The centre and farm are used mainly by schools, but guided tours can be arranged, as can joint visits with Enfield Butterfly Farm (see Animals).

For further information contact: Head of Environmental Education, Capel Manor Horticultural and Environmental Centre, Bullsmoor Lane, Waltham Cross, EN7 5HR (0992 763849).

Gardens of Capel Manor nearby (see Gardens).
Open throughout the year.

PICK-YOUR-OWN

You will have to follow the signposts in the summer to the farms and market gardens where you can pick your own strawberries, raspberries, currants, beans etc. Depending upon the rotation of crops not all farms have pick-your-own facilities every year. The following is a list of farms that operate regularly:

Aldenham: Blackbirds Farm
(09276 4940)
Bishop's Stortford: Hazel End Farm
(0279 813241)
Hertford: Bengeo Garden Centre, Bengeo
(0992 583464)
Letchworth: Manor Farm, Willian
(not available)
Potters Bar: New Cottage Farm, Enfield Ridgeway
(0707 43033)
Welwyn: Welches Farm
Burnham Green Road, Bulls Green (043879 769)

VINEYARDS

Frithsden Vineyard
Leighton Buzzard Road, Frithsden (0442 57902)
On the A4146. P

This is the only commercial vineyard in the county. It is situated on a 3-acre site on a S-facing slope on chalky soil with a flinty loam on top, similar to that found in the Champagne region of France. A light white wine similar to a Riesling is produced, as well as a rosé and a red wine. The harvesting team do not start gathering the grapes until late September, and picking goes on through October and in a good year even into November. Fermentation begins in the middle of October and finishes by the second week in December. The wine is then racked and filtered and is ready for bottling in March.

Conducted tours every Sunday, 10.45 a.m. School visits can be arranged.

Gardens

Gardens in Hertfordshire cover a wonderful variety from formal gardens like those at Knebworth, to specialized gardens such as the Gardens of the Rose at Chiswell Green, St Albans. Also included are some garden centres which have a special interest or offer a special service, and some town parks which have flower-beds and borders.

GARDEN CENTRES

For an exhaustive listing of nurseries and garden centres, readers should consult the relevant Yellow Pages telephone directory. The centres mentioned are selected from those which feature in directories and publicity material supplied by local authorities and/or tourist organizations.

Chorleywood: Highland Water Gardens
(09278 4135)
In Solesbridge Lane, next to the M25. P
A large water-garden centre; aquatic plants and ornamental fish on display.
March–September: Monday–Sunday, 9–5. October–February: weekends, 9–5.

St Albans: Ayletts Nursery
North Orbital Road, London Colney (0727 22255)
On the A414 P

A long-established nursery, Aylett has a wonderful display of plants, ranging from shrubs to pot plants to cut flowers. Advice on gardening problems freely available at advisory centre. A dahlia festival is held for 2 weeks in September, with glorious displays of floral art. Demonstrations are a regular feature at weekends and in the evenings.
Daily.

Stevenage: Roger Harvey Garden Centre
(0438 811777)
Bragbury End, S outskirts of Stevenage. P

Quality garden plants and products in historic farmhouse setting. Displays of shrubs, trees, roses and heathers. Wide range of garden machinery. Fencing, paving, garden buildings, patio furniture, ponds, barbecues; silk flowers; garden books; advice available from qualified landscape gardeners; house-plant conservatory, bottle gardens, hanging pots. For transporting large or heavy items, van available free of charge for local use. Children's corner, picnic tables, climbing-frame, collection of animals and pets, including 2 very small Shetland ponies; tanks of exotic fish; mid-week classes in flower arranging. School and group visits welcome. Informal Saturday talks and demonstrations given by well-known gardening personalities such as David Bellamy and Peter Seabrook. Country kitchen open every day for coffee, hot and cold lunches and teas. The emphasis is on wholesome home-made food in a farmhouse setting. Cornish cream teas.

Stevenage Lodge Horticultural Centre
Frobisher Drive, Chells P

An award-winning horticultural centre, opened by the

borough council in the house and grounds of Stevenage Lodge in 1979. It has well-laid-out leisure gardens, and provides a wealth of information on all horticultural matters for the keen gardener, as well as being a meeting-place for local horticultural and other organizations.
Daily: Monday–Friday, 9–4; weekends, 10–4 (October–March, 2–4).

TOWN AND COUNTRY GARDENS

See also Tewin: Tewin Mill Fish Farm and Water Garden in Animals.

Ashridge House and Garden (NT)
On the Ashridge Estate (see Countryside: Country Parks).
P
The park consists of nearly 4,000 acres. The gardens of the house (see Heritage: Historic Houses) were designed by Repton in 1814. There are extensive lawns, rhododendrons and fine trees.
April–October: weekends and BHs, 2–6.

Bishop's Stortford: The Castle Mound
Hockerill Road, Bishop's Stortford
The mound is thought to date back to the 10th century. It was the site of Waytemore Castle, which was built by William I, destroyed in King John's reign and demolished about 1649. Only a stretch of flint wall remains. The site eventually became the moated castle gardens consisting of flower-beds, tennis courts and a children's paddling-pool. Within the gardens are a day centre, a club for the aged and a scented garden for the blind.

Buntingford: Layston Court Gardens
Hidden from view, these gardens are reached by a footpath from the town's High Street or from the riverside footpath, known as 'Pig's Nose'.

The gardens originally belonged to Layston Court House, which was built in the early 17th century as Buntingford's grammar school. The gardens are now tended by Buntingford Council and during the summer months are the venue for local band concerts.

Chenies Manor Gardens

Chenies, Bucks (02404 2888)

Off the A404, the village of Chenies is on the B485, and a gravel drive leads from the village to the house.

Chenies Manor gardens are in harmony with the house. They are much frequented by painters, who are attracted by the riot of colour from the roses, lavender and other flowers bordering the York stone paths. There is a penitential maze, topiary work and an interesting physic garden where the plots are divided into sections – medicinal herbs, herbs for culinary use, poisonous herbs and sweet smelling ones. In a field adjacent to the garden are some Highland cattle. (For Chenies Manor House see Heritage: Historic Houses.)

Hatfield House Gardens

Hatfield House (07072 62823)

Hatfield House (see Heritage: Historic Houses) is 21 miles N of London on the Great North Road, A1000. P

The West gardens of the house date back to the late 15th century, when the palace of Hatfield was built. There were knot gardens, herbers, orchards and a privy garden, and probably a garden to grow vegetables.

Early in the 17th century, Robert Cecil employed John Tradescant the elder to plant and lay out the gardens. He went to Europe to bring back trees, bulbs, plants and fruit trees, many of which had not previously been grown in England. The great gardens designed for the first earl by the Dutchman Salamon de Caux, with their water parterres, grass knots and elaborate fountains, fell into decay in the 18th century, when landscaped gardening became fashionable.

The gardens have now been altered to try to re-create them as far as possible in their planting and design to have the feel of gardens of the 17th century, in sympathy with the great house which has changed so little. The lower W gardens have been completely redesigned, and there is a scented garden, a herb garden at its centre, and a great variety of sweet-smelling flowers, bulbs, trees and shrubs for every season of the year. The W Garden, enclosed by a yew hedge, is copied from an early plan found in the archives and is planted with many herbaceous plants, roses, irises and peonies and a great number of rare and unusual plants. A knot garden has been made in the courtyards of the palace. There is a foot maze planted in box and a historic collection of tulips and narcissi. Dogs not admitted to the gardens. Park: daily (except GF) 10.30–8. West Gardens: daily (except GF) 11–6; East Gardens: Monday only (except BHs), 2–5.

Hemel Hempstead: Water Gardens

Between the main car-parking areas and Marlowes, the main shopping street.

These delightful gardens, which come as rather a surprise in such a modern commercial setting, were designed by G. Jellicoe in the early 1960s and incorporate the River Gade in their design. Beds of shrubs, varieties of ducks on the lakes, an attractive fountain and huge formal flower-beds brighten the whole area. It is worth getting out of the car and walking along them to appreciate the colours and display.

Knebworth Gardens

Knebworth House (see Heritage: Historic Houses) P

The formal gardens were simplified in 1909 by Sir Edwin Lutyens and are now gradually being restored to their more elaborate Victorian design, including the herb garden, designed for Knebworth by Gertrude Jekyll. The

250 acres offer picturesque walks in the deer park.
April–early October: Tuesday–Sunday and BHMs, 11.30–5.30. House and gardens: 12–5.

Lemsford: Brocket Hall

An extensively landscaped park laid out by 'Capability' Brown with a series of waterfalls built on the River Lee. Public footpaths go through the park. (The house – formerly the home of Prime Ministers Lords Melbourne and Palmerston – is not open to the public.)

Rickmansworth: Basing House Gardens

Basing House (see Heritage: Historic Houses)
Access from the High Street or from the public footpath running beside the railway line.
Basing House Gardens are municipal gardens which surround a bowling-green.

St Albans: The Gardens of the Rose

Chiswell Green, St Albans (0727 50461)
On the outskirts of St Albans. Easy access from M1 and M25. Signposted in Chiswell Green. P
The gardens are run by the Royal National Rose Society, which is the country's oldest and largest specialist horticultural society. The Gardens of the Rose are the society's show ground and collection of 30,000 roses of all types. The 12 acres of garden are being continuously developed and are a magnificent spectacle. The British Rose Festival is a national event, held over a weekend early in July each year. Among the many attractions are a magnificent display of roses organized by the society and rose-growers on an exciting new theme each year. There is a competition for the leading national amateur rose-exhibitor and floral artist, and displays of handicrafts in great variety. Gift shop, licensed cafeteria. Dogs may be brought into the gardens on leads. Picnics are not allowed in the gardens. D

Mid-June–October: Monday–Saturday, 9–5; Sunday, 10–6. August BHM, 10–6. Evenings: parties by appointment only.
Fee

Stevenage: Benington Lordship Gardens
(0438 85668)
5 miles E of Stevenage. P
Lovely old hilltop garden on the site of a Norman castle (see Heritage: Castles). Ruins, lakes, herbaceous borders, rock and water garden, spectacular views, old and new roses, wide variety of shrubs and kitchen garden. Weather permitting, snowdrops can be seen on the last weekend in February and the following week, and on Sunday noon–5. Plant centre opens in May. Home-made teas on Sundays and BHs. Picnics welcome. Unsuitable for wheelchairs and the disabled. No dogs.
Easter and summer BHMs: 12–5. Last Sunday in April, May Sundays not followed by a BH, Sundays in June and July, and first Sunday in August: 2–5. Fee

Waltham Cross: Capel Manor Horticultural and Environmental Centre
Bullsmoor Lane, Waltham Cross P
These ornamental and educational gardens cover 25 acres. There is a lovely walled garden with old-fashioned roses, mixed herbaceous and shrub borders, a 17th-century knot garden with hedges and herbs, gardens with colour and texture themes, rock gardens, water gardens, ornamental fish and greenhouses with tropical and carnivorous plants. 5 acres are used for trials and demonstration gardens in association with *Gardening from Which?*. There are some fine specimen trees, including a copper beech which is 220 years old. Teas. For Capel Manor's other attractions, see Farms. D
For opening-times, ring 01 363 7288. Fee

Watford: Cheslyn Gardens

Nascot Wood Road, Watford (0923 226400, ext. 2501)

This house and garden were bequeathed to the Borough of Watford in 1965 by Mr Colbeck, a local architect who designed both the house and the initial layout of the garden, which has been altered over the years, with the addition of the rock garden. The whole area covers approximately 3½ acres and broadly comprises a woodland area and formal gardens near the house. There is an aviary containing 14 different species of birds in one corner of the gardens, and during the spring the woodland garden has a beautiful display of rhododendrons, azaleas and drifts of bulbs and bluebells. There is fine autumn colour. (The house is not open to the public.)

D

Daily: April–September, 10–8; October–March, 10–4.

Welwyn: St Paul's Walden Bury

(043887 218)

W from Knebworth, along country lanes.

The Bury is the birthplace of Queen Elizabeth The Queen Mother and the home of the Bowes-Lyon family. 18th-century formal woodland garden with temples, statues, lakes and ponds. Informal flower gardens.

Occasional Sundays.

TOWN PARKS

There are too many open spaces and recreation grounds in Hertfordshire to mention here, but below is a list of some of them. They vary considerably in size and recreational facilities. Some have formal flower-beds and borders, and some have tennis courts, paddling-pools and children's playground equipment.

Baldock	Weston Woods – natural amenity area; access from A6141

Bishop's Stortford	Castle Gardens
Borehamwood	Meadow Park, Brook Road (01 207 0870)
Chorleywood	Chorleywood House grounds
Hemel Hempstead	Water gardens
Hertford	Hartham Common, beside the canal Castle grounds
Hitchin	Priory Park Bancroft Park Windmill Hill Walsworth Common Butts Close
Hoddesdon	Barclay Park: dog-free area of swings and slides
Potters Bar	Oakmere Park Parkfield Open Space King George V Playing Field
Royston	Priory Gardens. Laid out by public subscription in memory of those who died in the Second World War.
St Albans	Abbey Orchard Verulamium Park Clarence Park Vintry Gardens
Sawbridgeworth	Pishiobury Gardens
Stevenage	Town Centre Gardens, King George V Park Fairlands Park Shephalbury Park Hampson Park, Webb Rise, Pin Green
Tring	Memorial Gardens

Ware	Priory Ground and Gardens
Watford	Cassiobury Park Gammons Lane Recreation Ground Garston Park
Welwyn Garden City	King George V Playing Fields Stanborough Park

Heritage

ARCHAEOLOGICAL SITES

Places of archaeological interest which are accessible to the general public are listed below, but in many cases the sites of archaeological finds have had to be converted to modern use and there is now nothing to be seen. Objects of interest have in most cases been placed in the appropriate local museums.

ANCIENT ROUTES

Ermine Street

The Roman road Ermine Street was built to link London with Lincoln and the north. The route is close to the A10, but there are stretches which still survive as track through woodland – e.g. the section between Wormley (N of Cheshunt) and Hertford Heath. The route is marked on the Ordnance Survey maps, and the old embankments and ditches can still be identified.

Icknield Way

The great prehistoric relic of the region is not a 'site' at all: it is Britain's oldest long-distance path – the Icknield Way, which connected the agricultural lands of East Anglia with the religious centres at Avebury and Stonehenge. Parts of it have been built over, but one of the best stretches still accessible to walkers is a 4–5-mile stretch from the B655 E of Pegsdon to the A6 N of Luton. Those interested should consult the walker's guide published by the Icknield Way Association (Membership Secretary, 19 Boundary Road, Bishop's Stortford).

INDIVIDUAL SITES

Ashwell: Arbury Banks

Access from Partridge Hill bridleway, S of the Newnham Way/Hinxworth Road junction, W of Ashwell.
An Iron Age rampart and ditch enclosing about 12 acres of farmstead. As so often, the outlines of the enclosure are probably more clearly visible from the air than from ground-level.

Graveley: Chesfield Church

From Stevenage, take the B197 to Graveley. At the garage, turn into Church Lane and continue along it for about 1½ miles to the remains of the church on the N side of the road near Chesfield Park.

This is one of a number of ruined medieval churches in the county. The records show that a church existed in 1216, but it probably pre-dates that time. Following amalgamation of Chesfield parish with Graveley in 1445, a licence to demolish the church was granted in 1750. The site, which is privately owned but can readily be seen from the road, has been recently tidied up. The ruins consist of a rectangular nave and chancel probably dating from the 14th century, plus a small later chapel at the SE corner.

Hemel Hempstead: The Highfield Barrow

On the W side of High Street Green, Hemel Hempstead, near the junction with Queensway.
This is a large, well-preserved burial chamber, but it is not

easy to see, as it is rather overgrown. It is considered to be of the Roman period rather than of earlier times.

Hexton: Ravensburgh Castle

Access by footpath S from the Hitchin to Barton road (B655) at Hexton.

An Iron Age hillfort some 20 acres in area. Not easily visible because the terrain is heavily wooded, but a good view is possible from the high point of the Hexton to Lilley road. The site is privately owned, but by prior arrangement (0582 881204) parties may visit it between February and April

Redbourn: The Aubreys

Travelling W on the B487 after Redbourn church, you find the Aubreys on the left just after the road passes beneath the M1. A footpath is signposted.

Aubreys is a big prehistoric plateau fort occupying over 20 acres, but although the circular earthworks survive, the fort is not easy to see at ground-level.

Royston Cave

Entrance in Melbourn Street, beneath a shop.

Discovered in 1742, Royston Cave is a bell-shaped chamber dug out of chalk, about 25 feet high and 17 feet in diameter. It dates from pre-Christian times and is also believed to have served as a Roman sepulchre and an oratory. There are crude carvings and coloured reliefs of saints, kings and queens of various dates. Broadsheet guide and postcards available. Parties can be shown round by arrangement with either the town council or the local history society.

Easter–September: weekends and BHs, 2.30–5.

Royston: Therfield Heath

Therfield is about one mile off the A10 S of Royston.

The site consists of 10 tumuli (burial mounds),

apparently grouped round a single long burial chamber, probably of the early Bronze Age. Roman relics found nearby are probably attributable to the close proximity of the Icknield Way. One mile W of this ancient cemetery is an Iron Age earthwork known as the Mile Ditches.

St Albans: Beech Bottom Dyke

From the city centre, take the Harpenden road (A1081); turn right at the Ancient Briton public house; fork left along Firbank Road and then left at the junction with Valley Road. The dike can then be seen on either side of the road.

The dike (a large ditch up to 30 yards wide and about 10 yards deep) has banks on both its N and S sides and runs for about a mile roughly W to E. It is thought that it was probably linked to Devil's Dyke at Wheathampstead and that the two are of much the same date (50–10 BC). Both were probably part of a dike system developed by the Catuvellauni tribe in the period preceding the invasion by the Romans in AD 43.

St Albans: Verulamium Park and Roman Theatre

W of the cathedral, off of the A414.

In the beautiful setting of what is now Verulamium Park is the site of the Roman city of Verulamium. The main features – walls, theatre, hypocaust – are clearly signposted.

Large sections of the Roman wall, including the London Gate, are still standing. The ruins include the hypocaust, a preserved mosaic floor of a building, showing the system of under-floor central heating by ducted hot air. Houses, shops, streets and temples occupied over 4 centuries have been excavated, and some parts are still visible above the ground. Parts of the 3rd-century Roman defences, with towers, ditches and gate foundations can also be seen. A roman theatre (off Blue House Hill) formed part of the city and has been excavated: it was unique, being a theatre with a stage, rather than an amphitheatre. It had an audience capacity of up to 2,000 people.

City walls etc: Daily.

Roman Theatre (0727 54051): Daily. Summer, 10–5.30. Winter, 10–4.

Hypocaust: Daily. March–October: Monday–Saturday, 10–5.30; Sunday, 2–5.30. November–February: 2–4. Fee

Stevenage: The Six Hills

The Six Hills lie on the W side of the London Road just to the SW of the roundabout where Six Hills Way and London Road meet.

Dating from towards the end of the 1st century AD, they are considered to be one of the finest surviving groups of Romano–British burial barrows in the UK.

Stevenage: Whomerley Wood

Within Whomerley Wood on the NW side of Fairlands Valley Park, about a mile SE of Stevenage centre.

These well-preserved earthworks of a typical medieval moated site can clearly be seen. Limited investigations of the site were carried out in 1924 and 1953, establishing fairly reliably that there was medieval occupation of the site.

Welwyn: Roman Bath House

Dicket Mead (07072 71362)

Underneath the A1(M), close to the Clock roundabout, reached from the Hertford road (A1000). The Bath House is the surviving section of what was originally an extensive collection of residential buildings dating from the 3rd century AD. What remains shows the layout of the cold, warm, hot and furnace rooms, and the hot and cold baths, plus parts of the hypocaust heating system. Exhibitions of finds from local archaeological excavations.

Sundays and BHs, 2–5 (or dusk).

Guided tours at other times by arrangement with the

curator at the Old Mill House Museum (see Heritage: Museums).

Wheathampstead: Devil's Dyke and The Slad

From the centre of Wheathampstead take the B653 Welwyn Garden City road for about ½ mile; turn right into Dyke Lane and continue for 150–200 yards; Devil's Dyke can then be found on the E side of the lane. Access is through an iron gate. The dike is about 500 yards long, 12 yards deep and about 40 yards wide at the top. Another earthworks system known as The Slad runs parallel to the dike, about 500 yards E. Expert opinion seems to differ as to whether the 2 structures formed part of the same defensive system, but the latest thinking is that Devil's Dyke was related not to The Slad but to the Beech Bottom Dyke and other dike systems.

CASTLES

Though numerous pre-Roman forts were built in Hertfordshire, the main outbreak of castle-building followed the Norman Conquest of 1066. At various dates, a number of castles were added to the original pair at Berkhamsted and Hertford – Anstey and Walkern, Benington and Waytemore (see Gardens for details of the 2 last-mentioned) – but apart from Berkhamsted and Hertford there remains little to see save dry moats and vestiges of flint wall.

Anstey Castle

In Anstey village just off the B1368 E of Buntingford, behind the church.

The earthworks of the Norman 'motte-and-bailey' castle. The motte, about 30 feet high, is encircled by a moat which is mostly still full of water. The bailey is in the private grounds of Anstey Hall.

Berkhamsted Castle (EH)
(04427 2411)
Near the railway station.
In December 1066, shortly after the Battle of Hastings, William the Conqueror arrived at Berkhamsted, where, to prevent an attack on London which could not have been withstood, the Saxon leaders offered him the crown. Soon after, work began on the castle, which remained an important stronghold until the end of the 15th century. Thomas à Becket lived there when he was Lord Chancellor, and Edward the Black Prince died in the castle. At different times it was the property of Catherine of Aragon, Anne Boleyn and Jane Seymour. In the reign of Elizabeth I it was leased to a Sir Edward Carey, who used some of the stones to build elsewhere. Little masonry is left today, but the earthworks are still impressive. The middle rampart is now a public walk. During the Second World War, many London statues were placed in the castle grounds for safe-keeping.
Daily: March–October, 9.30–6.30; November–February, 9.30–4.

Hertford Castle
In the town centre. (0279 55261, ext. 487)
In the year 905 King Edward the Elder built a castle on the E of River Lee, and this was probably the site of the later Norman castle which almost certainly dates from the reign of William I (1066–89). The gate-house was built in the 15th century and is still standing; otherwise only some wall fragments remain. It was at different times a prison for King John II of France, King David of Scotland, and Isabella, widow of Edward II. The gate-house, altered and extended over a period of 300 years, was given to Hertford Borough in 1906, since when it has been used as administrative offices.
Castle: first Sunday of month May–September, 2.30–4.30, when local councillors are present to show visitors round.
Grounds: Daily.

CHURCHES AND THE CATHEDRAL

Until recently, you could go into a church at any time of day or night, but because of vandalism and the theft of offertory boxes and church treasures, many churches are now kept locked except during times of worship and special services. It is usually possible to obtain a key by application to the verger or the priest in charge. A charge is often made for brass-rubbing.

St Albans Cathedral

On Holywell Hill.

This fine cathedral has been used for Christian worship longer than anywhere else in Britain. Until 1877 it was known as 'the abbey and parish church of St Albans', but by royal charter in that year St Albans became a city, and its parish church became a cathedral.

Alban was a Romanized Briton of some standing, and he was also a Roman citizen. He gave hospitality to a travelling Christian priest in the days when Christians were still persecuted, and he was converted by his visitor. He refused to renounce his new-found faith and was beheaded on 22 June in the year 208. In those days executions had to take place outside the city walls, and the hill SE of the Roman city of Verulamium was the site of his execution. When Christianity became accepted and its followers were no longer persecuted, the site became a shrine, and a monastic church was built there in the 4th century. It has been the focus of pilgrimages ever since.

A monastery was founded, supposedly by the Saxon King Offa of Mercia, in about 793. The abbey church was completely rebuilt by Paul of Caen in the 11th century, following the invasion of William the Conqueror. He used many bricks and materials from the site of Verulamium and incorporated some of the parts of the earlier Saxon church.

By 1700 the buildings were in a state of near collapse,

and only the choir and the area beneath the tower were used. Sir Edmund Denison Beckett, later Lord Grimthorpe (who also designed the clock and bell of Big Ben), came to the rescue with a large amount of money and provided the means for total restoration, provided he was given a free hand. He made many drastic alterations, some out of keeping with the original designs. It is still, however, a magnificent structure and, set at 320 feet above sea-level, the highest cathedral in England, it can be seen from afar. The nave is 300 feet long and is the longest in Europe. The Norman arches have the largest number of medieval wall-paintings surviving in the country, depicting crucifixions on the piers on the N side of the nave.

The actual shrine of St Alban was demolished at the time of the Dissolution of the Monasteries, but fragments found during work done in the 19th century have been reassembled in their original position in the Saint's Chapel behind the High Altar. This is what the throngs of pilgrims who made their way to the abbey in the Middle Ages would have come to see. This is where they would light their candles and kneel in prayer, watched by monks in a timber watching-chamber where a constant vigil was held.

(See also Arts and Crafts: Bell-Ringing.)

Ashwell: St Mary

Ashwell church can be seen from miles around. With its distinctive Hertfordshire 'spike' (a spire on top of a tower), it is one of the landmarks of N Hertfordshire. The tower itself is made from soft white limestone, called clunch and quarried locally. The elegant spire which crowns it is leaded. Most of the church was built in the 14th century. It has a long chancel and is rather bare, but as the tall Perpendicular windows are clear-glazed, there is a sense of light and space. The medieval graffiti are famous and are scratched on pillars in the N arcade and inside the tower. They are in Latin and comment on the Black Death in 1349 and on a storm and 'a mighty wind' in 1350; there is also a drawing in great detail of the spire of Old St Paul's Cathedral in London before it was destroyed by lightning in 1561. In many ways this church resembles that in Baldock but it is somewhat grander because of the local wealth from wool and the greater availability of local stone.

Ayot St Lawrence: St Lawrence

The 13th-century church was partially demolished on the orders of Sir Lionel Hyde because it spoilt the view from his new house (Ayot House, built in the 18th century). The bishop found out what he was up to and halted the demolition. The old church, which stands in the main street of the village, is now a picturesque ruin, and because it is in such a dangerous state the gates are kept locked. The church which Sir Lionel Hyde had built in its place, designed by Nicholas Revett and completed in 1779, is on the edge of the village. It looks like a Greek temple from a distance and in fact the Palladian front with its fluted columns was copied from the temple of Apollo at Delos and was designed to be a focus of interest from the big house. The inside of the church is beautifully proportioned and is much smaller than it appears from the outside. The small organ is the original one. The church now looks rather neglected.

Baldock: St Mary the Virgin

There are many similarities to the parish church dedicated to St Mary in Ashwell, although there is some evidence that this church was earlier. Like Ashwell's this church is light and spacious and has a 'Hertfordshire spike' (a tower capped by a small spire). There is a splendid set of 15th-century screens extending right across the chancel arch and the 2 broad aisles. Those who are keen on brass-rubbing will find some good ones here, including one depicting a man with a hunting-horn. There is a 13th-century marble coffin lid and an ornate Victorian memorial to Georgiana Caldecott, showing her with an angel carrying her soul up to Heaven.

Bengeo, near Hertford: St Leonard

This little Norman church was built around 1120 and has hardly been altered at all over the years. The roof would once have been thatched but is now tiled, and other changes which have been made have not spoiled the original appearance. The church is rectangular, with an apse at the east end. It is about 70 feet long, and its most interesting features are a Norman font, an anchorite's cell and some wall-paintings on either side of the chancel arch. The church is open for worship only on alternate summer Sundays.

Benington: St Peter

Most of this church was built in the 14th century but the tower is 16th-century and was restored in 1889. In the north wall of the chancel is a beautiful decorated arcade under which are the tombs of members of the Benstede family. There is some interesting detail here, including a lady with a wimple and a king pierced by a sword. Next to the green in the village is a cottage with a leaning timbered gable in which the priest lived until another rectory was built in 1637.

Brent Pelham: St Mary

Visitors come to Brent Pelham specially to see the little church, in whose N wall is buried one Piers Shonkes, said to be the last dragon-slayer in England. The story goes that in the reign of William the Conqueror Piers Shonkes killed a dragon that had been troubling the area, only to find that it was a particular favourite of the Devil, who vowed to have Shonkes's body and soul when he died, 'whether buried within the church or without'. To thwart the Devil, Shonkes was buried in the wall, and so his tomb was neither inside nor outside the church. The symbolism on the tomb undoubtedly depicts a dragon, among other things, but the sober view is that this is meant to represent militant Christianity. The tomb is considered by some authorities to date from the 13th century, while the Latin verse, the date 1086 and the name of Piers Shonkes were probably added some 3 centuries later. Still, it's a good story.

Bygrave: St Margaret

This simple country church is in proportion to the small village it serves, between Ashwell and Baldock. It consists only of a nave and chancel. The nave is strengthened with Roman bricks and tiles, and there is some detailed carving round the Norman doorway. There is simple tracery on the screen, and at the W end of the nave is a suitably rustic bell frame.

Cottered: St John the Baptist

The church is on the top of a hill in open country, so the leaded spire can be seen from afar. It was built in the 14th century and has no aisles. The tall Perpendicular windows make the church very light. An early painting of St Christopher, depicting some of the dangers of travel at the time, was discovered under a covering of whitewash, and part of it can now be seen on the N wall opposite the entrance to the church. The site may have been used at one time for pagan rites as a large stone has been incorporated into the base of the tower, and this is suggestive of earlier pagan use.

Flamstead: St Leonard

The 'Hertfordshire spike' (a tower capped by a small spire) on the massive tower of this church can be seen on the skyline. The tower consists of a strange mixture of materials – flint, stone, tiles, plaster and brick, including some Roman bricks. The base of the tower dates from the 11th century and the upper part from the 15th century. A clerestory (a series of high windows to let in more light) was added in the 13th century and damaged a series of early wall-paintings. Part of a large St Christopher was discovered during restoration work in the 1920s, and this can be seen above the N arcade. A 14th-century betrayal can be seen in the NE chapel. There are plenty of graffiti – including 3 epitaphs in verse to deceased parishioners carved on pillars in the nave. There are 2 interesting monuments: one to the Saunders children in 1690, and in the N arcade an altar tomb (*c.*1420) with effigies of a man and wife. On the chancel wall is an effigy in armour of the Master of the Household to Queen Elizabeth I, Sir Bartholomew Fowke.

Furneaux Pelham: St Mary the Virgin

Most of the church is late 15th-century, but some parts predate that period. There are 3 piscinas (stone basins for washing holy vessels) near the altar, and a brass in the Newport Chapel of about the time of Richard II. One of the bells dates from before the Reformation. The chapel contains stained glass by William Morris and Burne-Jones. The roof beams are supported by angels, dressed in scarlet, blue and gold and carrying musical instruments or heraldic shields. This paintwork was renewed in 1963–4. The church has a tall W tower, topped by a 'Hertfordshire spike' (a tower capped by a small spire) and carrying a clock which bears the motto 'Time flies. Mind your business.'

Hatfield: St Etheldreda

Located by the Old Hatfield Palace gate, this church is full of associations with the Cecil family. Most of it was constructed in the 13th century, but the W tower and the Brocket chapel are 15th-century. The Salisbury Chapel was built in the 17th century and contains the memorial to the first Earl of Salisbury; his effigy is supported by the 4 virtues above a skeleton. There is a stained glass window in the S transept by Burne-Jones.

Hemel Hempstead: Great St Mary

This is a fine Norman church and, as is common in Hertfordshire, has a central tower and a leaded spire. The building was completed in 1180, and restoration work carried out in 1880 and 1980 has not spoiled the character and style of this beautiful church. The central tower is supported by Norman arches, and there are similar arches on either side of the nave. This is the only church in the county to have a chancel with a vaulted roof, and the sacristy also has a rib-vaulted roof. The clerestory (high windows over the chancel to let in more light) is unusual in that it was inserted at the time of the original building. There are some fine brasses representing Robert and Margaret Albyn.

Hertford: Friends' Meeting-House

This building dates from 1669–70 and is the oldest purpose-built Quaker Meeting House in the world that has been in continuous use for worship since it was built. It is set back from the street, and there is a small garden at the rear. Both Robert George Fox (1624–91) the founder of Quakerism, and William Penn (1644–1718), who established the state of Pennsylvania in the United States, visited and worshipped there.

Hitchin: St Mary

The tower was built in the 12th century and is very low for the size of the church, most of which was destroyed in an earthquake in 1298. Hitchin prospered from the wool trade, so that when the church was rebuilt in the 14th century this increased affluence was reflected in the grander and more elaborate style of the new building. The tower, nave, chancel, aisles and splendid porch are all battlemented, and the porch is surmounted by 4 pinnacles. To the front of it are spaces and pedestals for 6 statues which were removed during Cromwell's time, when the faces of the Apostles round the font were also mutilated.

The beautiful screens of oak tracery enclosing the chancel chapels are the finest in the county. The church also contains a painting of 'The Adoration of the Magi' from the school of Rubens, and a 14th-century tile glazed with yellow lead under which is the portrait of a man who looks remarkably like the franklin in Chaucer's Prologue to the *Canterbury Tales*. There are some good brasses, and an ambulatory (an area for walking, as in the cloisters of a monastery) has been made behind the high altar.

King's Langley: All Saints

This is a handsome 15th-century church built of flint rubble and brick, and it has the characteristic Hertfordshire embattled tower and leaded spire. The walls of the chancel date from the 13th century. There is a double piscina (a stone sink for washing holy vessels) near the altar. In 1608 there was an order that 'a comely and decent pulpit' should be provided, and a new pulpit was then installed to comply with this requirement. There is a brass to John Carter dated 1588. He had 2 wives, one of whom had 4 sons and 5 daughters, the other 5 sons and 4 daughters. The church contains the tomb of Edmund of Langley, first Duke of York, and his wife Isabella. This had previously stood in the church belonging to a nearby friary of Dominicans but was moved to the parish church in 1575. It was opened in 1877 and was found to contain another skeleton as well, that of a lady of about 33 years. Another tomb is that of Sir Ralph Verney, whose father had been Lord Mayor of London in the 16th century.

Little Hadham: St Cecilia

A tree-lined path from Hadham Hall (now a secondary school) leads to this 15th-century church with its open, timbered porch. There is a graceful screen, and some box pews opposite a 3-decker pulpit dated 1633.

Little Hormead: St Mary

This is a lonely, isolated church with a magnificent N door showing what marvellous decorative ironwork the Normans could do. The roof is the original, and the nave has a plaster ceiling.

Much Hadham: St Andrew

Henry Moore, the sculptor, lived in this village and gave the heads of a king and a queen that decorate the W door. Apart from this modern touch, the church dates from 1225, when building began. It has the usual 'Hertfordshire spike' (a spire on top of a tower). The oak door of the N vestry has big 13th-century hinges; it was probably moved there from somewhere else. There are several brasses and two rare chairs with high backs and traceried panels that may once have been part of a 14th-century 3-seater sedile (a stone seat for priests beside the altar).

Northchurch: St Mary

St Mary's, in the Bulbourne valley, has a low but massive embattled tower and fine windows of stained glass. The present nave was the original church and has walls made of flint, but at the W end the wall is much thicker, suggesting that there was a separate room there for the priest. The N aisle, S porch and vestry were added in 1881, and the E window was designed by Kempe in 1883. A notice at the S end of the nave states that all the seats are for the 'free use of the parishioners according to the law'. There are some interesting brasses, including a portrait that looks like one of Socrates, and another commemorating the Reverend Samuel Noyes, who was prebendary of Winchester and rector of the parish for 32 years.

'Peter the Wild Boy' is commemorated in a brass memorial on the S wall. Peter was discovered – black-haired, brown-skinned and naked, except for a tattered shirt – in a field in Germany by Jurgen Meyer of Hamelin in Hanover. The burgomaster sent him to a hospital nearby, where he was found to be quite harmless. He was never taught to speak. Two fingers of his left hand were webbed up to the joint. George I (r.1714–27) heard about him and, at the instigation of the Princess of Wales, Peter was brought to Britain and placed in the care of Mr Fenn of Broadway Farm near Northchurch. He remained quite wild and used to wander in the woods wearing a leather collar with a brass rim inscribed 'Peter the Wild Man from Hanover. Whoever will bring him to Mr Fenn at Berkhamsted shall be paid for their trouble.' He died in 1785 and is buried just outside the porch.

St Albans: St Michael

The church is a simple rectangle with aisles that were added later. It is situated within the site of the Roman city of Verulamium, and materials from that city were used in the original construction. You can still see some of them in the N doorway into the chancel and in the quoins in the E corners of the nave. There is a splendid monument to Sir Francis Bacon of Gorhambury, depicted asleep in his chair. The artist is unknown, and the memorial was executed after the death of its subject in 1626.

St Albans: St Stephen

St Stephen's is also a Saxon church, and materials from Verulamium were used in its construction. A tiny restored window from the original church can still be seen in the N wall, but a Norman arch which has since been blocked off has cut into it. The church was largely rebuilt in the 14th century. The brass eagle lectern of 1480 came from Holyrood Abbey, Edinburgh.

St Ippolyts: St Ippolyts

This church has an unusual dedication but probably derives from the Greek story of Hippolytus, who was thrown from his chariot and dragged to death by his horses. Two medieval saints had the same name, and there seems to have been some local connection with horses, because it was said that all horsemen who went that way took their horses into the church, right up to the high altar. According to local folklore, when the Knights Templar left Temple Dinsley to go on the Crusades they would ride over to St Ippolyts to be blessed. Crosses cut in a pillar on the S aisle are supposed to have been made by them on their departure. The church was rebuilt in 1878, carefully using much of the old materials. A Norman window and door have been retained, and so have features from other architectural periods.

Wyddial: St Giles

The chapel and N aisle of this 14th-century church were built entirely of brick when they were added in 1532. Jacobean box pews were added later. The church contains 8 panels of 13th-century Flemish glass. There are brasses dated 1575 and 1546. The screen is 17th-century.

HISTORIC HOUSES

Ashridge House

Little Gaddesden (044 284 3491)

Off the B4506, 3 miles N of Berkhamsted.

A monastery was founded here in 1283 but became the property of the Crown when the Dissolution of the Monasteries took place. The present building was constructed by James Wyatt for the second Duke of Bridgewater and dates from the early 1800s, being a fine example of the neo-Gothic Revival. Of the former monastic buildings only a barn (much altered) and a crypt below the main block survive. The house is a management college and is only occasionally open to the public, but the gardens are open more frequently (see Gardens).

Ayot St Lawrence: Shaw's Corner (NT)

Ayot St Lawrence, near Welwyn (0438 820307) P

At the SW end of the village, 2 miles NE of Wheathampstead, approximately 2 miles from the B653.

This was the home of George Bernard Shaw from 1906 until his death in 1950. Many of his hand-written letters and manuscripts can be seen, as well as literary and personal mementoes. The rooms remain as in his lifetime, including the kitchen and pantry. A walk round the garden goes past the hut where he did much of his writing. D: limited access

April–October: Wednesday–Saturday, 2–6; Sunday and BHMs, 12–6. March–November: Wednesday–Sunday, 11–6 (except GF). Some delay on busy days. Group visits by written appointment only. Fee

Chenies Manor House

Chenies, Bucks (02404 2888)

Off the A404 on the B485 is the village of Chenies, and a gravel drive leads from the village to the house. P

Chenies Manor was once the home of the Duke of Bedford, but it was sold to pay death duties in 1954 and is now in private hands. The present manor dates from Tudor times. The house is in dark red brick, with a steeply pitched roof and tall decorative chimneys. Both Henry VIII and his daughter Elizabeth I stayed there. The furniture, tapestries and needlework blend with the charm of the manor house, and the gardens contain old English flowers and topiary work. There is a physic garden, an ancient well, secret underground passages, a reputed priest's hole and a dungeon. Shop, afternoon tea. D: gardens

April–October: Wednesday and Thursday, 2–5. Spring and August BHs, 2–6. Fee

Chorleywood: Chorleywood House P

The former home of Lady Ella Russell, a member of the

Bedford family. The house is now used as council offices. The grounds are a public open space with tennis courts. A Swiss-style chalet is used by a playgroup. The house is not open to the public but can be viewed from the outside.

Hatfield: Hatfield House

(07072 62823)

21 miles N of London, on the Great North Road (A1000). Easy access from M1 and A1. P

A magnificent Jacobean stately house built for Robert Cecil, first Earl of Salisbury and chief minister to James I. It has been the family home of the Cecil family ever since. World-famous paintings, fine furniture, rare tapestries and a collection of historic armour are on view in the various rooms. There is a high marble hall, minstrels' gallery, grand staircase and great screen with 5 carvings. Exhibits of Queen Elizabeth I's possessions are on view in the long gallery. Winter dining-room, library, armoury, chapel and kitchens. Coffee shop, gift and garden shops. See also Gardens.

March–October: Tuesday–Saturday (except GF), from noon; Sunday, 2–5.30. Easter, May, Late Spring and August BHMs, 11–5. Parties of 20 or more should book in advance. Fee

Hatfield: Old Palace

(07072 62055)

Only one wing of the original red-brick palace survives. Henry VIII's children Mary, Elizabeth and Edward spent much of their early childhood there. The Great Hall has a superb timbered roof of oak and chestnut. Elizabethan-style banquets are held in the hall throughout the year. During her sister Mary's reign, Elizabeth was virtually a prisoner here, and she is said to have been sitting beneath an oak tree when she received the news of her accession. See also Gardens.

(Not open to the public, except for private functions) April–December: Tuesday, Thursday, Friday and Saturday evenings (booking essential).

Knebworth: Knebworth House

(0438 812661)

Entrance direct from A1(M) at junction 7. Stevenage S A602. P

This has been the romantic and historic home of the Lytton family since 1490. It was transformed 150 years ago by a Victorian novelist into a fantasy with high Gothic towers. It illustrates English history over 5 centuries and is a much loved family home. Many beautiful rooms, including a magnificent state drawing-room, can be seen. Fort Knebworth and a large adventure playground. Gardens and park (see Gardens). Narrow-gauge steam railway.

Park: April–early October, Tuesday–Sunday and BHMs, 11.30–5.30.

House and gardens: April–early October, Tuesday–Sunday and BHMs, 12–5. Fee

Luton Hoo

Park Street, Luton, Beds (0582 22955)

2 miles S of Luton, between the A6 and A6129. P

Luton Hoo, surrounded by gardens and parkland, is the home of the famous Wernher collection, which includes paintings by Rembrandt and other Dutch masters, tapestries, porcelain and priceless Fabergé jewellery. It was begun in 1767 by Robert Adam for the Third Earl of Bute. Its 1,500 acre park was laid out by 'Capability' Brown. After fires, the house was remodelled in 1903 by Mewes for Sir Julius Wernher, the diamond magnate. Cafeteria, picnic area, shop.

Mid-April–early October, daily except Monday (unless a BHM): 2–5.45. Saturday, 11–6; Sunday, 2–6. Fee

Moor Park Mansion

Off the A404, in the middle of Moor Park golf course. P

The house once belonged to Cardinal Wolsey but after his downfall became the property of Henry VIII, who often used the manor. He granted it to Anne of Cleves after their divorce. It has had many famous owners since then. During World War II the mansion was requisitioned and became the headquarters of the first British Airborne Corps, who planned the Battle of Arnhem. In 1945 it returned to the golfers. The house has 14 bedrooms, besides reception rooms, fishponds, a stone-built lodge, dog kennels and orangery. The mansion was built in Palladian style with a magnificent portico on the W front. It is now the club house for 2 golf courses (see Sport: Golf). Guided tours on some days in summer months. Information from Three Rivers Council offices (0923 776611, ext. 51). D: limited access

Monday–Friday: 10–4. Saturday: 10–noon (except BHs).

Rickmansworth: Basing House

Access to the gardens from the High Street or from the public footpath running beside the railway line.

This building is not open to the public but is worth looking at from the outside, because of its historical interest. It was the home of William Penn, the famous Quaker statesman and founder of Pennsylvania. He lived here with his wife, Gulielma, for 5 years after their marriage in 1672. Their house was later used as a school and then was owned by a local doctor who started the fire brigade in Rickmansworth and was also renowned because he closed down 14 of the town's pubs in one day. It is now used as council offices. There are public gardens (see Gardens) and a bowling-green at the rear.

Rickmansworth: The Bury

Off Church Street.

This was the former manor house of Rickmansworth, and

the present building dates from the 17th century, although it has been altered considerably since then. The house is used as offices, but it can be seen from the outside, and the grounds are open to the public. A cut from the canal, which was used to deliver goods to the manor house, is still visible.

Rickmansworth: The Elms

High Street, Rickmansworth

The house was a summer residence of the Victorian novelist George Eliot (Mary Anne Evans), and it was here that she wrote *Daniel Deronda*. The house is not open to the public and is now part of St Joan of Arc's School.

Royston: Wimpole Hall (NT)

Arrington, Royston, Cambs (0223 207257)

6 miles N of Royston, off the A603 P

A spectacular mansion in 18th-century style. Rooms intimate and formal, with work by Gibbs, Flitcroft and Sone. 350-acre landscaped park includes a grand folly and a Chinese bridge. Walks through the park. Restored Victorian stable block with heavy horses. Shop, restaurant, picnic area. Young Visitors' Guide. D

The adjacent Home Farm (see Farms) is well worth a visit.

April–October: Tuesday–Thursday, weekends, 1–5; BHMs, 11–5. Fee

St Albans: Gorhambury

(0727 54051)

W of the A414, up a private drive beside the Roman theatre (see Heritage: Archaeological Sites).

Gorhambury is the home of Lord and Lady Verulam and was built about 1784. A fine example of a Georgian mansion, it is raised on a plinth and reached by a flight of broad steps with a projecting Corinthian portico. It has a magnificent great hall, Chippendale furniture, 16th-century enamelled glass and an unrivalled collection of family portraits.

May–September: Thursday, 2–5. Fee

Sawbridgeworth: Market House

On the corner of Bell Street and Knight Street.

This house is a good example of the Tudor houses found in this pretty town in E Hertfordshire. Its handsome oak beams are original; the old fireplace once had an open hearth, and the smoke was drawn up through vents in the roof. 17th-century panelling has been restored, and the garden still contains an oasting house, which leads one to assume that this may once have been a site for the local malting industry.

Sawbridgeworth: Pishiobury

The mansion of mellowing brick is set in a fine park of 250 acres and at one time belonged to Anne Boleyn. There is a lake beside the house which is approached by an avenue a mile long, now bordered by some houses. James Wyatt rebuilt the mansion in 1782. Another house, Falconers, was once the official residence of the falconer, and some of the wall panelling and other fittings came from the original Elizabethan manor house.

Ware: Place House

Bluecoat Yard, off East Street, Ware.

This was one of two medieval manor houses and is interesting because the main room is a hall which has aisles like a church, in order to increase its width and carry the weight of the extended roof beams. The hearth was in the middle of the floor. In 1674 Place House was bought by Christ's Hospital City of London School, and young children were sent there to enjoy the clean country air. Later the building was encased in brick, and a row of cottages was built on the W side of Bluecoat Yard. In 1970 it was acquired by the Hertfordshire Building Preservation

Trust and renovated. It was reopened by the Queen Mother in 1978.

OTHER HISTORIC BUILDINGS

Anstey: The Village 'Cage' or Lock-Up

The village lock-up in Anstey was made by enclosing part of the church lich-gate.

Ashridge Estate: Bridgewater Monument (NT)

At Northchurch, 3 miles N of the A41, just off the B4506. P
Forming part of the Ashridge Estate (see Countryside: Country Parks), which extends over 4,000 acres, this granite monument was erected in 1832 to mark the achievements of the great canal-builder, the third Duke of Bridgewater. It is 108 feet high. You can climb to the top, from where there are splendid panoramic views of Ivinghoe Beacon and the surrounding countryside. Shop, information centre. Tea kiosk open summer weekends.
April–end October: Monday–Thursday, 2–5; Saturday, Sunday and BHMs, 2–5.30. Fee

Ashwell: Village Lock-up

At the bend of Hodwell.
Built in 1800 with clunch blocks (soft white limestone) from the former chantry chapel in the old churchyard.

Barley: Village Cage

To the right of the gallows-type sign of the public house the Fox and Hounds. The village cage is small and rectangular.

Buntingford: Village Lock-up

Next to the Fox and Duck public house is a tiny lock-up. It was a said that a spout from the pub supplied the inmates with ale!

Cheshunt: Temple Bar Theobald's Park

This was designed by Sir Christopher Wren and replaced the earlier wooden structure which formed the gateway to the City of London. It caused such serious traffic congestion in the 19th century that is was dismantled and re-erected in Theobald's Park. The City of London has often tried to secure its return, but it still stands to this day, vandalized, neglected, very over-grown. You can reach it only on foot.

Cromer Mill

W of Buntingford; NE of Cromer Village, on the B1037.
This is a 17th-century post mill, whose exterior has been renovated. It is the only mill of its type in the country to have been fully restored.
Exterior only: at any time.

Croxley: Tithe Barn

Information: County Education Office (0923 226231)
On private farmland in Croxley Woods (see Countryside: Country Parks). Footpath marked on Ordnance Survey map.
This tithe barn was built between 1396 and 1401, when the abbey of St Albans owned the manor of Croxley, and the barn was used to store tithed produce. It is one of the largest in Hertfordshire, measuring 101 feet by 40 feet. The doors are large to admit a fully laden cart. There is a kingpost roof, and it is weather-boarded and tiled and stands on a flint-and-clunch base.
Open occasionally.

Digswell Viaduct

This viaduct was designed to carry the Great Northern Railway across the valley of the River Mimram. It has 40 arches and is 1560 ft long and 98 ft high above the river. The first train crossed the viaduct in 1850.

Oxhey Chapel

Built 1612 by Sir James Altham, Chancellor to Queen Elizabeth I. Original doors and roof beams. Open by arrangement with vicar. (01 428 3696).

St Albans: Clock Tower

At the end of French Row and the market-place.

The 15th-century clock tower is a 77-foot-high structure, originally a curfew tower, and offers splendid panoramic views over the city. An Eleanor Cross stood in front of the clock tower, one of the last resting-places of Queen Eleanor, wife of Edward I, on her long journey for burial.

GF–Mid-September: Saturday, Sunday and BHs, 10–4.30. Fee

St Albans: Fishpool Street

This was named after the monastery fishponds. It is a residential street with raised pavements and is full of architectural interest, with Elizabethan and Georgian houses. It was used by stage-coaches until 1827. The 800-year-old manor house of St Michael is now an hotel.

St Albans: French Row

This is a narrow medieval street formerly Cordwainers or Cobblers Row. In 1216 French soldiers were quartered in St Albans, to help the barons in their fight against King John. They were held prisoner in St Albans, and this is how the road got its name. It includes the Fleur de Lys Inn, built in the 15th century.

St Albans: Sopwell Nunnery

Sopwell Nunnery was completely demolished at the time of the Dissolution of the Monasteries. A private mansion was built here, probably using some of the materials from the original nunnery, but only a few ruins remain. There is an attractive view of St Albans Cathedral, and the ruins can be seen if you walk along the Ver-Colne Valley.

Shenley: Village Cage

A small beehive-shaped brick building in the High Street, this is one of several lock-up cages that survive in Hertfordshire. It was used for the over-night detention of drunks and other trouble-makers who would have appeared before the magistrate next day. On each side of the door is inscribed, 'Be sober, do well, fear not, be vigilant.'

Stanstead Abbots: Rye House Gate-House

Near Rye House Railway Station. P

This red-brick gate-house was built in the 15th century and is surrounded by a rectangular moat between the River Lee and the New River. It used to be part of the house, within the moat. In 1683 conspirators gathered in Rye House and plotted to assassinate King Charles II on his way back to London from Newmarket. The plot failed, and the conspirators were executed. In the 19th century, Rye House was part of a development of pleasure gardens, and the gate-house is once again part of a recreational area – the Lee Valley Regional Park (see Countryside: Country Parks). It now houses an exhibition which is open on summer weekends. Bird sanctuary run by the RSPB; Rye House motorcycle racing track.

Waltham Cross

When King Edward I's wife, Queen Eleanor, died in Lincolnshire in 1290, her body was taken in a funeral cortège which took 13 days to reach its destination, Westminster. At each overnight resting-place, King Edward I had a cross erected. The cross at Waltham stands not at the abbey, on the Essex side of the River Lee, where the Queen's body must have lain, but at the point where the road to the abbey left the London road. The cross has been very much restored and is now overshadowed by a huge new shopping centre.

Ware: The Gazebos

S side of High Street, Ware.

These riverside 18th-century summer-houses stand in the former gardens of coaching inns. Some are in a poor state of repair, but work is continuing to restore them to their former glory.

Ware: Priory

This was built from the remains of a Franciscan priory founded by the lord of the manor in 1338. After the Dissolution of the Monasteries it became a private dwelling-house. During the 1914–18 war it was used as a hospital for wounded troops, and in 1920 Mrs R.B. Croft, the owner, gave it to the people of Ware. Ware Town Council now act as trustees. The priory grounds are fully open to the public and include gardens, a play area, open-air swimming pool, bowling-green and putting-green.

Ware: Scott's Grotto

E Herts Leisure Services Centre, Scotts Road, Ware (0279 55261)

A remarkable folly, created about 1766 by John Scott, Quaker poet and friend of Dr Johnson, the grotto consists of underground passages, linking 6 rooms,and extends some 67 feet into the hillside. The walls are covered with flints, shells and pebbles. The grotto is unlit, and a torch is necessary.

Open by appointment with E Herts Leisure Services, usually Thursday and Saturday afternoon.

Watford: Old Free School

St Mary's churchyard, Watford.

In these days, when the history and organization of schools are a matter of political controversy, it may be of interest to many to view Mrs Fuller's Free School – the forerunner of Watford Grammar School – and to read the words carved in stone over the doorway of this charming building, which is surmounted by a cupola. The inscription reads as follows: 'Anno Dm. 1704. This free school was built and endowed for the teaching of poor children at the proper cost of Mrs Elizabeth Fuller of Watford Place the only daughter of Mr John Comyne alias Chilcott of Tiverton in Devonshire and of London Merchant who dyed ye 11th of November 1709 aged 65. Silvester Chilcott Gent. Brother to the foundress of this school has made an addition of £20 a year for ever.' Silvester Chilcott died in 1716 and was buried in the churchyard just outside the school which he had endowed in perpetuity.

MUSEUMS AND ART GALLERIES

General and Local Interest

Ashwell: Village Museum
Swan Street, Ashwell
Depicts village life from the Stone Age to the present day; housed in a timber-framed building. Shop.
Sunday, BHs: 2.30–5. Parties at other times by arrangement. Fee

Bishop's Stortford and District Local History Museum
Cemetery Lodge, Apton Road, Bishop's Stortford (0279 72257) P
In cemetery, SW of town centre.
Local archaeology and history displays. Shop. May–September: Friday, 10–4. First Sunday in the month and BHs, 2–6. At other times by appointment.

Bushey: Local Studies Centre
Church House, Rectory Lane, High Street, Bushey
Bushey Museum Trust make available a wide range of

local records for research and interest. Shop, research facility.
Tuesday, 7–10 p.m.

Chalfont St Giles: Chiltern Open-Air Museum
Newland Park, Gorelands Lane, Chalfont St Giles, Bucks (02407 71117) P
Historic buildings which would otherwise have been destroyed have been dismantled and re-erected in this open-air museum. They date from the 16th to the 19th century and are on view in 45 acres of beautiful parkland. A nature trail runs through the site. There are regular demonstrations by blacksmiths, lacemakers, potters, cartmakers, corndolly-makers and other craftsmen. Home-made teas, gift shop, picnic area, nature trail.
April–October: Wednesday, Sunday and BHs: August: Wednesday, Sunday, 2–6. Fee

Hatfield: Old Mill House Museum and Mill Green Watermill
Mill Green (07072 71362)
At Mill Green on the junction of the A1000 and the A414 between Hatfield and Welwyn Garden City. P
A local history museum in the home of millers who worked the adjoining water mill. Displays illustrating local life from prehistoric times to the 20th century. The mill has been restored to working order and is on show during the museum opening-hours. Flour is milled every Tuesday, Wednesday and Sunday. Shop, Research facility. D
Tuesday–Friday: 10–5. Weekends and BHs, 2–5.

Hertford Museum
18 Bull Plain, Hertford (0992 52686)
Collections of local archaeology, history, geology and natural history. Exhibits of the Hertfordshire Regiment. Publications for sale. D
Tuesday–Friday: 10–5. Saturday: 10–1, 2–5.

Hitchin: Museum and Art Gallery
Paynes Park, Hitchin (0462 34476)
Next to the library. P
Displays showing the social development of Hitchin. Exhibits from the Herts Yeomanry Trust, costumes and natural history exhibits. Programme of art exhibitions. Publications for sale. D
Monday–Saturday: 10–5.

Hoddesdon: Lowewood Museum
Lowewood, High Street, Hoddesdon (0992 445596)
In the High Street, in front of the Civic Centre. P
2 galleries have a display of artefacts, photographs and pictures, bringing local history to life. A third gallery has a programme of changing exhibitions of local and general interest. Part of the original gardens remains and is open to the public. The aviary houses a number of budgerigars. Shop.
Wednesday, Saturday: 11–5. Parties at other times by arrangement.

Letchworth: First Garden City Heritage Museum
296 Norton Way South, Letchworth (0462 683149)
Originally the drawing office of the architects Parker & Unwin, this museum depicts the history and development of Letchworth as the world's first Garden City. Publications for sale. D
Monday–Friday: 2–4.30. Saturday: 10–1, 2–4.

Letchworth: Museum and Art Gallery
Broadway, Letchworth (0462 685647)
In the Town Square. P
Displays of local natural history and archaeology, and discoveries from the Iron Age and Roman Britain. Publications for sale.
Monday–Saturday: 10–5.

Much Hadham: Henry Moore's House

This was the home of the famous modern sculptor, with exhibits pertaining to his life and work.

May–September: Monday–Thursday. (027984 2566 for appointment)

Rickmansworth Museum

(0923 771542)

In the old council chamber at the rear of council offices.

This is a small exhibition of local memorabilia, with a changing presentation of items, documents and photographs from local collections.

Royston: Royston and District Museum

Lower King Street, Royston (0763 42587)

This museum shows items collected by the local history society, illustrating the history of Royston and the surrounding area. Shop. D

Wednesday–Saturday: 10–5.

St Albans: Museum of St Albans

Hatfield Road, St Albans (0727 56679/66100, ext. 2427)

Easily reached from the M10, M25, M1 and A1(M). Follow signs for city centre. P

The museum illustrates the long history of St Albans, from the departure of the Romans to the present day. The Salaman collection of hand tools is displayed, using reconstructions of wheelwrights' and coopers' workshops and a sawpit.

'The Story of St Albans' exhibition recounts the history of the city over 1,000 years, including coaching and roads, the abbey, the ecological background, markets and fairs, railways and the growth of commuting. The museum maintains and displays material relating to the plant and animal life of Hertfordshire and collects information on its geological and landscape history. Shop. D

Monday–Saturday: 10–5.

St Albans: Kingsbury Watermill Museum

St Michael Street, St Albans (0727 53502) P

A 16th-century cornmill showing exhibits of old farm implements and machinery. Shop.

Tuesday–Saturday: 10.30–5. Sunday: 12–5.

Stevenage Museum

St George's Way, Stevenage (0438 354292)

In the undercroft of St George's Church. P

The museum tells 'The Story of Stevenage' from prehistoric times to the present day. Includes local geology, fossils, mammals, birds and live fish. Shops. D

Monday–Saturday: 10–5.

Ware Museum

The Priory Lodge, High Street, Ware (0920 67868/61261)

Opposite St Mary's Church. P

Displays on 'The Story of Ware' and aspects of the town's social history, industry and archaeology. Shop.

Summer weekends: 11–5. Parties at other times by arrangement.

Watford: Museum and Art Gallery

194 High Street, Watford (0923 32297)

In lower High Street, E of main shopping area. Next to High Street station. P

Local history of the area, from the earliest archaeological periods up to the present day. Displays on brewing, printing and paper-making, and printing-ink manufacture, which historically formed an important part of the life of the area. The picture gallery houses a changing programme of works by local artists, including Herkomer and Dr Munro's Bushey Academy. Shop.

Monday–Saturday: 10–5.

Weston: Country Museum and Craft Centre

Howell's Farm, Weston.

Housed in a 17th-century barn.
All year: Wednesday–Friday, 10–11.30, 3–6. Easter–December, weekends, 10–6.

Special Interest

Bishop's Stortford: Rhodes Memorial Museum and Commonwealth Centre
South Road, Bishop's Stortford (0279 51746) P
The museum is the birthplace of Cecil Rhodes. It contains details of his early years in Bishop's Stortford and a pictorial exhibition of his life and career in South Africa.
Monday, Wednesday–Saturday, 10–4. Tuesday, 10–noon. Closed first 2 weeks in August. Fee

Harpenden: Railway Museum
Luton Road, Harpenden
A private collection of thousands of small railway relics, including working signals.
Open only on certain BH weekends.

Hitchin: British Schools Museum
41 Queens Street, Hitchin (0462 59956) P
A Victorian classroom setting, illustrating the history of popular elementary education from 1800. Shop, research facility.
Open by appointment.

London Colney: Mosquito Aircraft Museum
Salisbury Hall, London Colney (0727 22051)
1½ miles from junction 22 of the M25, on the B556. Signposted. P
Exhibits including the historic de Havilland Mosquito aircraft, built at Salisbury Hall in 1940, and many other de Havilland aircraft housed in hangars. There are also extensive displays of aeronautical memorabilia, including medals, uniforms, air-raid precaution equipment, photo-

graphs, leaflets, aircraft radios and other equipment, covering the period through World War I up to today. Current aircraft productions are displayed in workshops. Shop. D

Easter–October: Sunday, BHs, 10.30–5.30. July–September: Thursday, 2–5.

St Albans: Organ Museum

320 Camp Road, St Albans

Entrance between Camp School and the telephone box. Bus S2 stops outside.

This museum contains fairground and mechanical dance-hall organs which formed the private collection of Charles Hart, who in 1978 made them available to the public on a permanent basis. Shop. Light refreshments during Sunday performances.

Sunday: 2.15–4.30, when a continuous programme of live music is offered. Visits by organized groups at other times are welcome by appointment. For further details telephone Harry Smith (09277 64786), Keith Pinner (0727 73896) or Eric Cockayne (0727 52875).

St Albans: Verulamium Museum

St Michaels, St Albans (0727 54659)

Adjacent to the A4147. P

Some of the finest examples of Roman mosaics and wall plaster have been excavated and reconstructed and are displayed in the museum. Many of the domestic utensils of daily life in the Roman period are on show – kitchen implements, craftsmen's tools, furnishings, fittings, religious items, jewellery, coins, pottery etc. Shop.

See also Heritage: Archaeological Sites.

April–October: Monday–Saturday, 10–5.30; Sunday, 2–5.30. November–March: Monday–Saturday, 10–4; Sunday, 2–4. Coach and school parties should book in advance to avoid overcrowding. Fee. Free to local residents

Stevenage: ICL Historical Collection

Cavendish Road, Stevenage (0438 313361) P

A fascinating collection and archive relating to the history of the computer.

Open by appointment.

Tring: Zoological Museum

32 Akeman Street, Tring (044282 4181)

Akeman Street is a turning off the High Street. P

Tring Museum is renowned for its magnificent collection of mammals and birds, which include nearly every kind of large mammal and countless different kinds of birds. There are also many reptiles, fishes, insects and other invertebrate animals. The museum was built at the end of the last century to house the valuable collections belonging to Lionel Walter, second Baron Rothschild. He commissioned experienced naturalists to collect animals for him from all over the world, and he selected only the finest specimens for display. Tring Museum was bequeathed to the nation in 1938 and forms an annex of London's Natural History Museum. It is a major centre for bird research as well as a popular venue for school parties. Shop. D

Monday–Saturday: 10–5; Sunday, 2–5. Fee

Ware: Museum of Street Lighting

Concrete Utilities Ltd, Great Amwell, Ware (0920 2270) P

Collection of 115 columns and lanterns, restored and erected, plus an indoor section of smaller items, dating back to 200 BC. D

Open by appointment

Welwyn: Roman Bath House

(07072 71362)

Beneath the A1(M) access from A1000 roundabout. P

A 3rd-century domestic bathing site (see Heritage: Archaeological Sites) with a display of objects excavated locally. Shop. D

Sunday and BHs: 2–5, and by appointment. Fee

The Market-Place

AUCTIONS AND MARKETS

Berkhamsted Middle Road (044286 5169)	Every Wednesday fortnight	Antiques, general furniture and effects
Bishop's Stortford Northgate End (0279 51388)	Thursday (weekly)	General household effects
	Tuesday (monthly)	Antiques
Hertford Castle Hall (0992 582249)	Usually 2nd Thursday in the month	Antiques
Hertford Cattle market (0992 582249)	Monday	Auction of general effects, household goods, bric-à-brac
Hitchin Old Market Place (0462 32018)	Tuesday	Produce and poultry

Tring Brook Street (99682 6446)	Every Saturday fortnight	Antiques, modern furniture and effects
Watford Watford Auction Rooms, Water Lane (0923 55322)	Saturday every month	General furniture and effects

CATTLE ETC

Hertford Caxton Hill Norris & Duval (0992 582249)	Monday, Thursday	Cattle, sheep, pigs, poultry, eggs, flowers, vegetables and other farm produce
Tring Brook Street Brown & Merry (99682 6446)	Monday	Livestock etc

GENERAL

Baldock	Wednesday	High Street
Berkhamsted	Saturday	High Street
Bishop's Stortford	Thursday	North Street
	Saturday	Corn Exchange (small market)
Bovingdon	Saturday	On the airfield
Buntingford	Monday	Market Hill

Hatfield	Wednesday, Saturday	Market-Place
Hemel Hempstead	Thursday, Friday, Saturday	Market Square
Hertford	Saturday	Caxton Hill
Hitchin	Tuesday, Saturday and BHMs	Old Market-Place
Hoddesdon	Wednesday	High Street
Rickmansworth	Saturday	Station car-park
Royston	Wednesday, Saturday	By Corn Exchange
St Albans	Wednesday, Saturday	St Peters Square
Stevenage	Thursday, Friday, Saturday	Multi-storey car-park off St George's Way
Ware	Tuesday	Kibes Lane car-park
Watford	Tuesday, Friday, Saturday	Charter Place

SPECIALISTS

Bovingdon On the old airfield	Saturday	Large number of stalls selling bric-à-brac, clothing, crockery, hi-fi equipment, car accessories, meat, jewellery, fabrics and soft furnishings
Hitchin Old Market-Place (0462 56202)	Friday, Thursday	Small market selling antiques, crafts, second-hand goods, bric-à-brac etc
St Albans First floor, Old Town Hall	Monday	Sale of jewellery, paintings, clothes etc.

WOMEN'S INSTITUTES

All WI markets are open every week except the fortnight immediately after Christmas.

Baldock Baldock Community Centre, Simpsons Drive	Friday, 9.30–11.30 a.m.	Preserves, home-baking, craftwork, garden produce and plants
Barnet Barnet Stall Market, St Albans Road	Saturday, 8–12.30	Mostly home-baking and preserves, some garden produce and plants

Berkhamsted Outside Boots in High Street Market	Saturday, 7.30–11.30 a.m.	Sells home-baking, preserves, garden produce, garden flowers and a good variety of herbs and less common plants
Bovingdon Memorial Hall, High Street	Saturday, 10–11.30 a.m.	Home-baking and preserves, usually plenty of garden produce, flowers and a good variety of plants, craftwork; also serves coffee
Buntingford The White House, High Street	Saturday, 8–11 a.m.	Home-baking and preserves, plants, garden produce and flowers
Cuffley Cuffley Hall Foyer, Maynards Place	Thursday, 9.30–noon	Home-baking and preserves, garden produce, flowers, some plants, craftwork
Harpenden Methodist Church Hall, High Street	Friday, 9–11.30 a.m.	Home-baking, preserves, garden produce, plants, flowers and craftwork

Hatfield Market-Place	Saturday, 8.30–1	Home-baking, preserves, garden produce and flowers, good selection of plants
Hertford Foyer of Castle Hall	Friday, 9.30–11.30 a.m.	Home-baking, preserves, garden produce, flowers, plants, craftwork
Hitchin West Alley Market	Saturday, 8–11.30 a.m.	Home-baking, preserves, garden produce, flowers and plants
Kings Langley Oddfellows Hall, High Street	Thursday, 10–noon	Home-baking, preserves, garden produce and plants, some flowers, craftwork; also serves coffee
Little Hadham Village Hall	Thursday, 12.30–3	Home-baking, preserves, garden produce and plants, wide range of craftwork
Redbourn Village Hall, High Street	Thursday, 9.30–11.30 a.m.	Home-baking, preserves, garden produce, plants, flowers, craftwork; also serves coffee

Royston Corn Exchange, Market Hill	Wednesday and Saturday, 8–noon	Home-baking, preserves, garden produce, plants, flowers, crafts

The Corn Exchange was being revamped at the time of writing and while work continues WI market will have a stall in the open market.

St Albans Methodist Church Hall, Marlborough Road	Saturday, 8.30–11.30 a.m.	Home-baking, preserves, wide variety of plants, garden produce and flowers
Sawbridgeworth Church House, Vantorts Road	Friday, 1.45–3.45	Home-baking, preserves, some plants and garden produce, craftwork
Ware Place House, Bluewat Yard, an interesting historic building	Friday, 9.30–noon	Home-baking, preserves, garden produce, plants and flowers, very wide selection of craftwork; coffee served
Welwyn Church House, Church Street	Thursday, 8–11 a.m.	Home-baking, preserves, garden produce and plants, flowers, craftwork; coffee served

Sport and Leisure

The great majority of sporting activities are covered by the facilities provided at the big sports centres (see Sport and Leisure Centres). Sports which are catered for extensively outside these centres have a separate section to themselves. The objective of this chapter is to point the reader in the right direction and to give some idea of what is on offer, not to provide exhaustive treatment of a well-nigh inexhaustible subject.

ADVENTURE PLAYGROUNDS

Hemel Hempstead

Adeyfield	Turners Hill
Bennetts End	Rant Meadow
Long Chaulden	Shrub Hill

Stevenage

Bandley Hill	Featherstone Road
Canterbury Way	St Nicholas Play Centre
Canyon	Shackleton Spring
Chells	Eliot Road
Pin Green	Hampson Park, Webb Rise

ANGLING

The fishing season lasts from mid March to mid June. The rivers, lakes, gravel pits and reservoirs of Hertfordshire abound with all sorts of fish – carp, pike, tench, roach, chub, barbel, trout etc. Fishing rights on some stretches of water have sometimes been given to angling associations, and in some places you have to obtain a licence from a water authority. Many towns have a fishing-tackle shop, and details of permits required can usually be obtained from these. Here are some of the places where you can fish.

Bishop's Stortford	River Stort; River Lee in the Lee Valley Park
Hertford	Towpath of the River Lee from Hertford; lock to Hertford Gauge
Radlett	Aldenham Country Park
Rickmansworth	River Chess, River Gade, River Colne, Grand Union Canal, Aquadrome
Stevenage	Fairlands Valley Park
Tring	Tring Reservoir
Ware	Towpath of the River Lee; Priory Gardens
Watford	River Colne, River Gade, Grand Union Canal
Welwyn Garden City	Stanborough Lakes

The Grand Union Canal is used extensively by anglers over much of its length. The British Waterways Board leases the fishing rights to the London Angling Association, which is also responsible for the day-to-day management of angling on the canal. Day tickets are issued by the association but a licence from the Thames Water Authority is also required. These are usually obtainable from the local fishing-tackle shop, which can usually also give details of the required permits. There is plenty of roach in the canal as well as perch, carp, gudgeon and bream. The best stretches of the canal are round Rickmansworth, Hunton Bridge, Toovey's Pounds and Northchurch Pound and in Tring Cutting.

TROUT FARMS

Many trout farms welcome visitors, and this can be an entertaining and interesting experience. Most farms are set in unspoiled river valleys, and some encourage visitors to walk around the ponds and permit them to feed the fish. Many trout farms have shops which sell fresh trout as well as frozen food and pâté. Some have leaflets giving advice on how to cook fresh and smoked trout for all occasions. If you are going to visit a trout farm, ring first to make sure it is open and to receive instructions on how to get there. You can usually hire a rod and buy flies.

Much Hadham: Gingercress Fish Farms
(027984 2225)
See also Animals.

Royston: Shepreth Mill Trout Farm
Shepreth Royston (0763 60351)

Tewin: Tewin Mill and Fisheries Ltd
Kingsbridge, Tewin, Welwyn Garden City (043871 6019)
See also Animals.

FLYING

Learning to fly is probably not as expensive as you think, and it's good fun and a real challenge. There are several flying schools in and around Hertfordshire where you can take up this leisure pursuit. They include the following:

Denham School of Flying
Denham Aerodrome, Tilehouse Lane, Denham (0895 833327)

Leavesden Flight Centre
Leavesden Airport, Watford (0923 671411)

London School of Flying
Elstree Aerodrome, Elstree (01 953 4344)

Panshanger School of Flying
Panshanger Aerodrome, near Hertford (0707 335021)

GO-KARTING

Bovingdon: Bovingdon Aerodrome
There are regular meetings on the disused runways of the airfield on Sunday afternoons during the summer months.

Hoddesdon: Rye House
There is a specially designed karting track behind the greyhound track. It is open for practice all week, and there are competitions and races at weekends.

GOLF

MUNICIPAL AND PUBLIC COURSES

Bovingdon: Little Hay Golf Course
Box Lane, Bovingdon (0442 833783)

Cheshunt: Cheshunt Park Municipal Golf Course
Flamstead End, Cheshunt (0992 24009)

Elstree: Elstree Golf Club
Parkfield, Watling Street, Elstree (01 207 5680)

Rickmansworth: Rickmansworth Public Golf Course
Moor Lane, Rickmansworth (0923 771542)

St Albans: Batchwood Golf Course
Batchwood Hall, St Albans (0727 33349/52101)

Welwyn Garden City: Panshanger Golf Club
Welwyn Garden City (0707 33350)

PRIVATE CLUBS

Aldenham: Aldenham Golf and Country Club
Radlett Road, Aldenham (09276 7775)

Ashridge: Ashridge Golf Club
Ashridge (044284 2244)

Berkhamsted: Berkhamsted Golf Club
The Common, Berkhamsted (04427 5832)

Bishop's Stortford: Bishop's Stortford Golf Club
(0279 54027)

Boxmoor: Boxmoor Golf Club
18 Box Lane, Boxmoor (0442 42434)

Brookmans Park: Brookmans Park Golf Club
(0707 52487)

Bushey: Hartsbourne Country Club Ltd
Hartsbourne Ave, Bushey Heath (01 950 1133)

Bushey: Bushey Golf and Squash Club
High Street, Bushey (01 950 2283)

Bushey: Bushey Hall Golf Club
Bushey Hall Drive, Bushey (0923 225802)

Cheshunt: Cheshunt Golf Club
Park Lane Cheshunt (0992 29527)

Chorleywood: Chorleywood Golf Club
Common Road, Chorleywood (09278 2009)

Essendon: P.L. (London) Golf Club
Bedwell Park, Essendon (0707 42624)

Hadley: Old Ford Manor Golf Club
Old Ford Lane, Hadley (01 440 9185)

Harpenden: Harpenden Golf Club
Hammonds End, Harpenden (05827 2725)

Harpenden: Harpenden Common Golf Club
Cravell's Road, East Common, Harpenden (05827 68257)

Knebworth: Knebworth Golf Club
(0438 812752)

Letchworth: Letchworth Golf Club
(0462 683203)

Moor Park: Moor Park Golf Club
Moor Park (0923 773146)

Oxhey: Sandy Lodge Golf Club Ltd
Sandy Lodge Lane, Oxhey (09274 25429)

Potter's Bar: Potters Bar Golf Club
Darke's Lane, Potters Bar (0707 52020)

Puckeridge: E Herts Golf Club
(0920 821978)

Radlett: Porters Park Golf Club
Shenley Hill, Radlett (09276 6262)

Royston: Royston Golf Club
Baldock Road, Royston (0763 42696)

St Albans: Verulam Golf Club Ltd
226 London Road, St Albans (0727 53327)

Stevenage: Stevenage Golf Centre
Aston Lane Aston (043888 389)

Totteridge: S Herts Golf Club
Tottteridge (01 445 0117)

Watford: W Herts Golf Club
Cassiobury Park, Watford (0923 36484)

Welwyn Garden City: Welwyn Garden City Golf Club
Mannicotts (0707 325243)

Wheathampstead: Mid Herts Golf Club
Wheathampstead (058283 2242)

Ranges
Watford: Watford Golf Driving Range
(Unigolf Ltd), Sheepcot Lane, Watford (0923 675560)

ICE-SKATING

Stevenage: Roaring Meg
London Road, Stevenage (general: 0438 740750; programme: 0438 741341) P
There are varying opening-times for children, under-5s accompanied by parents, families, disco nights etc. Price reductions for group bookings. Children's birthday parties. Licensed Bar, cafeteria with menu ranging from snacks to full meals. Skate shop.

KITE-FLYING

Some of the local authority parks and recreation grounds are very suitable, and so are areas of common land mentioned in the Countryside chapter. Here are a few suggestions:

Berkhamsted Common
Bovingdon Aerodrome
Chorleywood Common
Dunstable Downs, near Tottenhoe, Beds
Harpenden Common
Letchworth: Norton Common
Rickmansworth Aquadrome
Royston: Therfield Heath
St Albans: Verulam Hills, Verulam Park
Stevenage: Fairlands Valley Park
Welwyn Garden City: Stanborough Park, Mardley Heath
Wheathampstead: Nomansland Common

Further advice may be obtained from the British Kite Flying Association (0442 41221)

RIDING

There are plenty of opportunities for riding in the county. It is best to contact your local riding stables to find out about the cost of instruction and the hire of a pony or horse. There are riding schools and pony-trekking facilities at: Aldenham, Baldock, Broxbourne, Chorleywood, Colliers End, Cuffley, Hatfield, Hemel Hempstead, Little Gaddesden, Much Hadham, Rickmansworth, Sarratt, Tring and Welwyn Garden City. For details consult your local Thomson Directory or Yellow Pages. For general information and advice apply to: The British

Horse Society, British Equitation Centre, Kenilworth, Warwicks (0203 696697).

In parks and woodland you should keep to the marked bridleways. You should invest in suitable clothing if you are going to take up horse-riding. Hard hats are essential, in case you fall and hit your head. If you do not want to buy riding-boots, you should wear a strong, closed-in shoe with a small heel (trainers are not suitable). Trousers should be stretchy and loose fitting. Tracksuits are ideal; jeans tend to rub.

SPORT AND LEISURE CENTRES

The range of activities catered for varies from centre to centre, and it is advisable to enquire which of them provides the sport/activity in which you are interested.

Bishop's Stortford: Bishopsport Sports Hall
Boys High School, London Road (0279 55261, ext. 488)

Borehamwood: Nicholas Hawksmoor Centre
Cowley Hill, Borehamwood (01 953 8267)

Bricket Wood Sports Centre: Smug Oak Lane
Bricket Wood, St Albans (0923 662224)

Bushey: Hartspring Centre
Park Avenue, Bushey (0923 33039)

Cheshunt: Grundy Park Leisure Centre
Windmill Lane, Cheshunt (0992 31921)

Harpenden Sports Centre: Rothamsted Park
Harpenden (0582 767722)

Hatfield: Hatfield Sports Centre
Travellers Lane, Hatfield (07072 68769)

Hemel Hempstead: Dacorum Sports Centre
Park Road, Hemel Hempstead (0442 64822)

Hoddesdon: John Warner Sports Centre
Stanstead Road, Hoddesdon (0992 445375)

Letchworth: Fearnhill Sports Centre
Icknield Way West, Letchworth (0462 676017)

Letchworth: N Herts Leisure Centre
Baldock Road, Letchworth (0462 679311)

London Colney: London Colney Recreation Centre
Alexander Road, London Colney, St Albans (0727 22447)

Potters Bar: Furzefield Centre
Potters Bar (0707 57026)

St Albans: Batchwood Hall
Batchwood Drive,
St Albans (0727 44250)

St Albans: Westminster Lodge Leisure Centre
Holywell Hill, St Albans (0727 65800)

Stevenage: Stevenage Leisure Centre
Lytton Way, Stevenage (0438 316291)

Stevenage: Stevenage Bowl
Danestrete, Stevenage (0438 729538)

Ware: Drill Hall Sports Community Centre
Amwell End, Ware (0920 3242)

Watford: Watford Leisure Centre
Woodside Park, Horseshoe Lane, Garston (0923 671020)

Welwyn Garden City: Gosling Stadium
Stanborough Road, Welwyn Garden City (0707 331056)

SWIMMING

INDOOR POOLS

Bishop's Stortford: Grange Paddock
(0279 52322)

Borehamwood: Hertsmere Centre
Elstree Way (01 953 1274)

Buntingford: Ward Freeman
(0763 72566)

Bushey: Grange Park School
Falconer Road (01 950 6497)

Cheshunt: Grundy Park
Windmill Lane (0992 23345)

Hatfield: Hatfield Swimming Pool
St Albans Rd. West (07072 64487)

Hemel Hempstead: Dacorum Sports Centre
(0442 64822)

Letchworth: N Herts Leisure Centre
Baldock Road (0462 679311)

Potters Bar: Furzefield Centre
Mutton Lane (0707 57026)

Rickmansworth: William Penn
Shepherds Lane (0923 771050)

Royston: Green Plunge
(0763 42395)

St Albans: Bricket Wood Sports Centre
(0923 662224)

St Albans: Westminster Lodge
Holywell Hill (0727 65800)

Sawbridgeworth: Leventhorpe
(0279 722490)

South Oxhey: James Altham
Little Oxhey Lane (01 421 0211)

Stevenage: Leisure Centre
St George's Way (0438 313293)

Ware: Fanshawe Pool
(0920 66967)

Watford: Hempstead Road
(0923 21409)

Watford: Leggatts School
(0923 674812)

OPEN-AIR POOLS

Berkhamsted
Lower Kings Road (044286 4006)

Broxbourne: Lido
(0992 442841)

Bushey: King George V Recreation Ground
(01 950 3177)

Harpendon
(0582 767722)

Hertford
Hartham Common (0992 461592)

Hitchin
Fishponds Road (0462 4475)

Hoddesdon
High Street (heated) (0992 461592)

Letchworth
Norton Common, Icknield Way (0462 4673)

Tring
Tring Park School, Mortimer Hill (044 282 2353)

Ware: Priory Lido (heated)
(0920 60703)

Welwyn
Stanborough Park (heated) (043871 22833)

WATERSPORTS

CANOEING, BOATING, SAILING, WATER-SKIING, WINDSURFING

The following is a list of some of the places where you can find instruction in, or take part in, aquatic sports. It is sometimes a requirement that you can swim before you are accepted for a course on sailing.

Aldenham: Aldenham Country Park
(01 953 9602)
Signposted from the A5 and A41.
The lake was hand-dug by French prisoners of war between 1795 and 1797, and the purpose originally was to maintain the level of the surrounding rivers following the construction of the Grand Union Canal. Sailing is permitted with Aldenham Sailing Club. (See also Countryside: Country Parks.)

Broxbourne: Lee Valley Leisure Park
The Boat Centre, Old Nazeing Road (0992 462085)
Follow the A1170 to central Broxbourne and turn right down Station Road (B194)
Hire a rowing boat, or an electric motor boat or a traditional-style narrowboat. Take a picnic. Go on a trip on *The Pride of Lee,* a 52-seat waterbus. (See Countryside: Country Parks.)
Monday–Friday: 9–4. Saturday: 9–6. Sunday: 9–7.

Letchworth: N Herts Leisure Centre
Baldock Road, Letchworth (0462 679311)
There is a canoe club resident here.

Rickmansworth: Aquadrome
Part of the Colne Valley Park. (See also Countryside: Country Parks.)

Access from Harefield Road off the A404. P
There are 2 lakes, the Bury Lake and the Batchworth Lake. No public use of lakes for swimming or for own craft; rights to sail and water-ski are let to private clubs. Windsurfing school on Batchworth Lake. Model Yacht Club sails Sunday mornings on Bury Lake. Provision can be made for disabled/cars to be admitted to the Aquadrome grounds.
Chess Sailing Club: 0442 215916
Water-Skiing Club: 0923 777418
Windsurfing Club: 0923 771120
April–August: 8–8. September–March: 8–sunset.

Stanstead Abbots: The Marina
South Street, Stanstead Abbots (0920 870499)
Narrowboats, cruisers and rowing-boats for hire. Mooring and boat repairs.

Stevenage: Fairlands Valley Park
Six Hills Way, Stevenage (0438 353241)
The sailing lake is open to the public throughout the year. Bosun, gull, topper, sailboard boats for hire. Dinghies and boards can be booked in advance. Sailing courses are organized during the summer months. The Fairlands Valley Sailing Centre is a recognized sailing school. You can use your own canoe, sailing dinghy or sailboard on the main sailing lake but not a boat more than 14 feet long. A Challenger trimaran is available for handicapped sailors. Paddle-boats, canoes and rowing-boats are available for hire on the children's boating-lake during the summer. (See also Countryside: Country Parks.)

Tring: Cowroast Marina
(044282 3222)
You can hire a narrowboat on a weekly basis from here.

Watford: Cassio Wharf

By Cassio Bridge roundabout, A412. (Bookings and information: 043871 4528)
Public trips every Sunday afternoon from Ironbridge Lock in Cassio Bury Park. School trips arranged. Narrowboat *Arcturus* available for charter. Discount for senior citizens and handicapped groups.

Welwyn Garden City: Stanborough Lakes

The N Lake has rowing boats for hire. Junior canoes available for younger children. Part of the lake is sectioned off for model boats. The S Lake is used for sailing and windsurfing. You can use your own boat or sailboard (a launch fee is charged). Equipment for hire. Approved sailing and windsurfing courses for all ages. Special courses during the school holidays. Watersports shop. (See also Countryside: Country Parks.)

Towns and Villages

The towns which are included here have historical backgrounds, and many have buildings of interest. The villages have been chosen for similar reasons: some because they are pretty, others, such as Ashwell, because they present a picture of village life from the earliest times.

TOWNS

Baldock

Baldock derived its name from the old French word for Baghdad, which was given to it by the Knights Templar, who protected pilgrims from bandits in the Holy Land during the Crusades. They were granted the land here in about 1250 and established the town on its present site. (A town existed here in the Iron Age and in Roman times but it was then E of the Clothall road. That area has now been covered over by a housing estate.) Baldock stands at the crossroads of 2 ancient highways, the Icknield Way, and the Great North Road. Some of the old coaching inns known to travellers are still there. In the 13th century prosperity came mainly from the wool trade, and in the 18th century from Baldock's important position on coaching routes.

Look at:

Elegant Georgian houses in the High Street.

Wynne's Almshouses in the High Street: 6 houses of red

brick endowed in 1623 by John Wynne, 'who hath left a yearly stipend to every poor of either house to the world's end'.
St Mary's Church (see Heritage: Churches).

Berkhamsted

Berkhamsted derived its name from Bercheamstede (=hill homestead) and is on the Watford–Tring–Aylesbury Road – the Roman road called Akeman Street. Saxon nobles came out from London and offered the crown to William of Normandy here, rather than have him march on London.

Look at:
The castle (see Heritage: Castles). You can see the castle beside the station as you speed by on an inter-city train.
St Peter's Church.
Some old coaching inns: The Bull (16th-century), The Crown, The Swan and the Queen's Arms (all 17th-century).
The Victorian Gothic town hall built 1859, now an attractive shopping arcade.
Berkhamsted School in Castle Street – attended by Graham Greene, founded in 1544 by Dean Incent, whose overhanging half-timbered house is in the High Street, almost opposite the church.

Bishop's Stortford

'The town on the ford by the River Stort' was given by William I to the Bishop of London. Its population is now 23,000, and it has very good access to London, via the M11 and British Rail into Liverpool Street. It is also close to Stansted Airport, which is developing into London's third airport. Cecil Rhodes, the founder of Rhodesia (now Zimbabwe), was born at the Old Vicarage and educated at the Old Grammar School; his achievements are commemorated in the Rhodes Memorial Museum (see Heritage: Museums).

Look at:

The Boar's Head: a 16th-century half-timbered public house.
The Corn Exchange with its neo-Greek front designed by a local architect, G. Perry.
St Michael's parish church.
The Castle Mound (see Gardens).

Broxbourne

Right on the E side of Hertfordshire and bordering Essex, Broxbourne is part of a development from Wormley through to Hoddesdon. The High Road which runs through all these towns dates from the 16th century. Most of the housing is modern.

Look at:

The ruins of a 19th-century mill next to the entrance of Lee Valley Regional Park (see Countryside: Country Parks). St Augustine's Church. The Monson almshouses built of red brick in 1728: they have now been converted into flatlets for aged widows.

Hertford

4 rivers join at Hertford: the Lee, the Beam, the Mimram and the Rib. The highest navigable point of the River Lee is in the centre of the town, at Lee Navigation, where there is a small flotilla of barges and boats. This river once played an important part in the transportation of grain and flour to London. The Normans built the castle soon after the Conquest (see Heritage: Castles) and the motte and bailey can still be seen. The impressive gate-house, built in the 15th century, remains at the entrance to the castle grounds. Many buildings in the town have fine examples of pargeting (decorative plasterwork on the front).

Look at:

St Leonard's Church, Bengeo (see Heritage: Churches)
Friends' Meeting-House in Railway Street (see Heritage: Churches).
St Andrew's Street, full of antique shops.

The Old Verger's House, dating from 1450, in St Andrew's Street.
The cattle market (see The Market-Place).
The Salisbury Arms Hotel, a Tudor courtyard inn (see Eating and Drinking).
The Barge public house by the canal.
The Folly, a beautifully maintained group of 19th-century cottages.
Shire Hall, Fore Street, built in 1767–89 by James Adam, brother of Robert Adam.

Hitchin

Hitchin stands on the River Hiz but probably derives its name from 'Hicce', the Anglo-Saxon tribe who once inhabited this hollow in the downs. It is one of the most attractive towns in Hertfordshire and is a good example of how to preserve an old market town. Markets are still held (see The Market-Place) but only a small part of the huge market area that in medieval days extended over much of the site now covered by shops remains. The shopping area is traffic-free and retains a great deal of old-world charm.

Look at:
The museum, next to the library (see Heritage: Museums).
Old houses in Sun Street, High Street, Tilehouse Street and Bucklersbury.
The Biggin, in Biggin Lane. Built in 1600 on the site of a Gilbertine priory, it became an almshouse in 1723 for 'poore auncient and middle aged women'.
The Coopers Arms in Tilehouse Street, a coaching inn that retains some of its medieval features.
The Skynner's Almshouses in Bancroft, dating from 1670 and 1698

Letchworth

This was the first of the Garden Cities and incorporated the villages of Letchworth, Willian and Norton in its

5,000-acre estate. In 1898 Ebenezer Howard published a book called *Garden Cities of Tomorrow*, and he conceived the idea of a town with tree-lined streets, lawns and rose gardens, fountains and tall trees, and with a self-sufficient community. Industrial areas, civic buildings and commercial enterprises do not intrude into the residential districts.

Look at:

The museum, in a thatched house in Norton Way S (see Heritage: Museums).

The Leisure Centre (see Sport).

Royston

The Romans constructed Ermine Street nearly, 2,000 years ago as one of the great roads leading to their northern forts and defences. A settlement grew up where it crossed Icknield Way, another of their main roads, and at the intersection Lady Roysia of Newsells in the parish of Barkway erected a cross. It became known as Roysia's Cross, and later as Roysia's Town and then Royston. The stone upon which the cross stood now stands on the island next to the ancient crossroads. James I often stayed here because the open land around reminded him of the Scottish moors. The remains of the Old Palace used by him as a hunting lodge can still be seen in Kneesworth Street, as part of the rear of a gabled house. Opposite is Royston Museum (see Heritage: Museums).

Look at:

The parish church of St John the Baptist (see Heritage: Churches).

Royston Cave (see Heritage: Archaeological Sites).

The Bull Hotel, dating back to 1520, was one of 50 coaching inns of which only 8 survive.

The Priory Memorial Garden (see Gardens).

Therfield Heath (see Heritage: Archaeological Sites).

St Albans

Over 2,000 years of history have shaped the city of St

Albans, the oldest town in the county. After being defeated by Julius Caesar in 54 BC, the people of the late Iron Age moved to Prae Wood, W of the present town, and they actually minted some coins there. The Romans came back in AD 43 and on the slopes of the River Ver below Prae Wood founded the city of Verulamium, whose remains can still be seen. Today the site of the ancient city is partly public parkland and partly still under farmland. Many of the finds from excavations can be seen in the Verulamium Museum.

In AD 209 Alban, who was a man of some standing and a Roman citizen, refused to deny his Christian faith and was beheaded on a hill outside the city, as was then the custom. A shrine was built on the spot once Christianity was accepted, and there has been a church there ever since. St Albans was the premier abbey in England in the 12th century. It still dominates the town and is still a centre for pilgrims.

In 1800 the town still did not extend far beyond the streets immediately surrounding the abbey, but it has grown substantially this century, with modern housing developments and new industries. With improved communications, it is also a commuter town.

Look at:

The abbey (see Heritage: Churches).

The site of the city of Verulamium (see Heritage: Archaeological Sites).

Verulamium Museum (see Heritage: Museums).

The town centre, including the Clock Tower and French Row (see Heritage: Other Historic Buildings).

The shopping centre and market (see The Market-Place).

The Gardens of the Rose at Chiswell Green (see Gardens).

Kingsbury Watermill, St Michael's Street (see Heritage: Museums).

The Organ Museum (see Heritage: Museums).

Gorhambury House (see Heritage: Historic Houses).

Ayletts Nurseries (see Gardens).

Sawbridgeworth

This town has retained its old-world charm in spite of modern development. It is cradled on the River Stort in some of the prettiest countryside in the county. A settlement may have existed here in the late Ice Age, as a flint hand-axe from that period has been discovered. Pottery from Roman times has also been excavated. 2 of the fine roads built by the Romans pass near the town and are now modern highways: Stane Street (N) and Ermine Street (W). The spelling of the town name has varied in documents through the years, but it was recorded as 'Sabrixteworde' in the Domesday Book and in Old English meant 'the settlement beside the bridge made of withies' (willow).

Look at:

The parish church of Great St Mary whose spire can be seen from afar.

The conservation area which protects nearly all the old town buildings, from the timber-framed ones to the many fine Georgian shops and houses.

Sayesbury Manor, owned by Geoffrey de Say in 1189.

The many paths and lanes leading to open spaces and river banks.

Pishiobury (see Heritage: Historic Houses).

Rivers Nursery, reputed to be the oldest in England.

Market House (see Heritage: Historic Houses).

Fair Green, where 2 annual fairs are held.

Some of the old inns: The Old Bell, The Queen's Head, The Good Intent, The White Lion (see Eating and Drinking) and the William IV, with its unusual handpumps.

Tring

Tring was founded by the Saxons, who found a gap in the Chiltern Hills beside the stream at New Mill, but it remained no more than a hamlet until the construction of the canals and the coming of the Rothschild family in the

20th century. It is a busy little town, and new housing estates are filling in the gap to the railway station, which is 2 miles from the centre of the town.

Look at:

The parish church in the town centre (see Heritage: Churches).

Tring Reservoir (see Countryside).

Go to:

Pendley Manor (see Arts and Crafts).

Tring Museum (see Heritage: Museums) and all the lovely Rothschild houses round the museum.

Hastoe, a tiny hamlet in the woods S of the town, near the highest point in the Chiltern Hills.

The cattle market, one of the only 2 now in Hertfordshire (see The Market-Place).

Walk:

One part of the Ridgeway, through Pavis Wood to the Crong, through splendid beech woods.

Ware

'Ware' means 'weir'. The town stands on the River Lee, and King Alfred probably built the first river-crossing. In medieval times Ware and Hertford were rivals and used to damage each other's fords and bridges in order to harm trade. In those days Ware had the better location, standing on the old Ermine Street which became the Great North Road, and thus had better communications for the local malting and milling industries. These industries have now gone, and the A10 bypasses the town, but many of the streets and buildings are of historic interest.

Look at:

St Mary's Church in the High Street. In it is the marble tomb of Sir Richard Fanshawe, statesman and poet of the 17th century. The font in the church is very beautiful, the carvings depicting saints and angels, some playing musical instruments.

Place House, perhaps one of the manors mentioned in the

Domesday Book. It was later used as a school for boys of Christ's Hospital who were being fostered in Ware (see Heritage: Historic Houses).

Scott's Grotto (see Heritage: Other Historic Buildings).

VILLAGES

Albury

This village is in the NE of the county, adjoining Essex, and is not to be confused with Aldbury on the other side of the county, nearer Buckinghamshire. It is a tiny village on the River Ash, a tributary of the River Lee at Ware. The village consists of little more than an inn and a church, which has a 'Hertfordshire spike' (a spire on the top of a tower) and a tomb dated about 14th century which has been mutilated. A house on the edge of the churchyard dates from the 15th century and may at one time have been the home of the priest.

Aldbury

Not to be confused with Albury in E Herts, this lovely village lies at the foot of the magnificent beechwoods of Ashridge Common. Its centre has been unspoilt by modern housing developments, and timber-framed houses on either side of the village street lead to a pond, a stocks, a whipping-post, and even space to park your car. The huge old elm tree by the pond succumbed to Dutch Elm Disease – a young oak has now replaced it. The village green is a popular background for films and television productions. The church, with its high tower, was restored in the 19th century. In a glass case inside is an old pitch pipe, used to give correct pitch for singing. There are two attractive public houses, the Greyhound and the Valiant Trooper (see Eating and Drinking), and tea-rooms.

Aldenham

This small village is just off the busy road between Watford and Radlett and has not, therefore, been spoilt by through traffic. The parish church of St John the Baptist has had an interesting development. Blackbird's Farm is one of the most popular pick-your-own farms and has a popular farm shop (see Farms). Nearby, Aldenham School was founded in 1596, and another famous school, Haberdashers' Aske's, was founded on the original buildings of Aldenham house, built about 1700.

Anstey

There was once a castle at Anstey (see Heritage: Castles), but all that remains is the motte (mound), upon which it was built, and the moat, which is mostly filled with water. There is a moat, too, round the rectory, and on a farm E of the site of the old castle is another mound with a moat round it. The church of St George is one of the few cruciform churches in the county, i.e. shaped like a cross. Part of the lich-gate was enclosed to make a village lock-up (see Heritage: Other Historic Buildings).

Ashwell

Right in the N of the county and bordering Cambridgeshire, Ashwell presents a comprehensive picture of village life, from the days when there was a settlement in the Iron Age and a hill fort giving an outlook over the Icknield Way, to the present day, when it is a popular commuting village for people working in Cambridge and the capital. E of the village is a gully of ash trees where the River Rhee rises, and stepping-stones cross the spring. The magnificent tower of the parish church of St Mary topped by its graceful spire (see Heritage: Churches) can be seen for miles around. The graffiti scratched on the church walls date back to the time when the church was built and are miniatures of village people. All sorts of styles and types of houses stand side by side in the streets: thatched, timbered, gabled, red brick and some of yellow brick, following a terrible fire in the last century. The building which was the local tithe office in the 16th century is now the museum (see Heritage: Museums). If you want to spend some time looking at this charming village, there are plenty of places to get something to eat (see Eating and Drinking).

Ayot St Lawrence

The word 'Ayot' may be derived from the name of the valley that once lay between the two villages, Aega's Gap. Undisturbed by modern roads and traffic jams, this little village can be reached by narrow lanes in lovely wooded countryside. The remains of the ruined church are overgrown with trees and ivy (see Heritage: Churches) and are closed to the public because they are unsafe. The new St Lawrence Church was built in 1778 in its place (see Heritage: Churches). The village is probably best known for its association with George Bernard Shaw, whose home is open to the public (see Heritage: Historic Houses). The Brocket Arms sells food and drink (see Eating and Drinking).

Ayot St Peter

Even smaller and more remote than its sister village, Ayot St Peter is less of a tourist attraction. One or two fine buildings are set in parkland: Ayot Bury was built in 1672, and Ayot Place was once a timber-framed farmhouse built in about 1615. The church has a fine carved pulpit.

Barkway

A milestone in the village gives the distances to London and Ware, and Barkway was a regular stopping-place in the days of horse-drawn traffic. Many of the cottages have been restored, some with grants from the Hertfordshire

Preservation Trust, and with its thatching in apple-pie order and the lovely pond beside the churchyard and the Manor Farm, the village has a picture-book appearance.

Benington

The Normans built a moated mound with a stone keep here and then demolished it about 40 years later. The manor house remained, and a mock castle was built alongside it in the 19th century. There are some beautiful gardens on the site of the Norman castle Benington Lordship Gardens (see Gardens). The village which grew round the mock castle is very pretty, with timbered cottages spaced round the village green. The cottage with the leaning gable was the priest's house until the Old Rectory was built in 1637. The parish church of St Peter is very beautiful, with some fine stone corbels (see Heritage: Churches). The churchyard is famous for its display of snowdrops in the spring.

Bramfield

Drastic restoration of the church, with its tiny tower and spire, in the mid 19th century, made it almost totally Victorian. Thomas à Becket, murdered in Canterbury Cathedral in 1170, was the first rector of Bramfield. Woods managed by the Forestry Commission surround the tiny village. Some of the old buildings are very attractive, with some timber-framed thatched cottages and a 17th-century public house, the Grandison Arms, named after a lord of the manor.

Chipperfield

This attractive village has a beautiful and well-cared-for cricket pitch bordered on 2 sides by the woods of the Common (see Countryside: Country Parks) and on the other 2 by many interesting houses. The tiny old village school opposite the flint church has now been converted into small dwellings, but there are many grander ones both round the green and tucked away in the woods. The village is busy in the summer months, with picnickers, walkers and people watching the cricket. The public house and hotel facing the green, the Two Brewers, is popular all the year round, doing excellent lunches and bar food, and is one of the few places that still serves afternoon tea, in Wedgwood china, in the very agreeable lounge.

Flamstead

The name is probably a corruption of Verlamstead, 'refuge on the River Ver'. It is on a hilltop W of the Ver Valley, and the spike on the tower of the church of St Leonard (see Heritage: Churches) is a landmark on the horizon. Old houses surround the church, including the row of brick Saunders Almshouses built in 1669. The Bury, or local manor house, is very nearly in Redbourn and is now a farmhouse. The former village school is now a private dwelling but can still be seen behind the church. Unspoiled by busy roads, the village retains its quiet and rural atmosphere.

Great Amwell

In 1800 Robert Mylne designed some beautiful water gardens in this village. They can be seen just below the parish church of St John the Baptist, and the combination of islands in the river, weeping willow trees and the sweep of the river makes a delightful and romantic setting, one of the most beautiful spots in the county. The gardens were designed to commemorate the venture of Sir Hugh Myddleton in 1609 when he created a new river which carried fresh water from springs in the vicinity to a reservoir (the New River Head) in Clerkenwell. From there the water was piped through mostly wooden pipes to supply fresh water to people living in the north of the capital.

Great Gaddesden

This village, tucked away in beautiful Chiltern countryside, lies in the Gade river valley. Houses and cottages are clustered round the church. Roman bricks were used in the buttresses of the tower. The village is overlooked by Gaddesden Place on the top of the hill. This was built in 1763 but was destroyed by fire in 1905 and has been restored. It has been the home of the Halsey family since the 16th century. The artist Gordon Beningfield often used Great Gaddesden (and Little Gaddesden, nearby) as the background for his wildlife paintings.

Great Hormead

In the E of the county, this little village retains much of its old-world charm with timbered and thatched cottages. The moat of the 16th-century hall can still be seen. The little church is mostly 14th-century but had extensive restoration in 1873.

Great Wymondley

There had been a Roman settlement here, and a Norman lord used some of the earthworks to construct a motte (mound). Just W of this, a church was built at the same time. There is a tiny green with some 17th-century cottages beside it. The farm called Delamere House was built in the 16th century and was added to later. The manor house opposite the public house, the Green Man, is also 16th-century. A row of small 17th-century thatched cottages, Hornbeam Court, is especially attractive, having been recently restored.

Kelshall

This village is in the N of the county and has fine views over great expanses of arable land. There is a Georgian rectory which is very handsome, and the village also has 2 crosses. The church of St Faith gives some idea of what churches used to look like when they were decorated with wall-paintings.

Kimpton

Set in a valley lying E/W, this ancient village has a long main street with some interesting buildings, and some modern housing estates. The church of St Peter and St Paul is set above a tower upon a hill to the N. It has the needle spire above a tower commonly seen in this county, fine arcades with some beautiful moulding on the columns, and some interesting brasses (see Arts and Crafts: Brass-Rubbing.)

Little Amwell

The Roman road of Ermine Street passes through this village which has extended with new housing development to Hertford Heath, where there is a nature reserve. When the architect, William Wilkins, was 27 years old, he was engaged to design a building to be used as a training school for employees of the East India Company. When this was wound up in 1857, it became a public school, Haileybury College. Wilkins went on to design the National Gallery in Trafalgar Square, and you can see the similarity. Haileybury College is not open to the public but is of interest for its historical and architectural history. It can be seen just S of Hertford Heath.

Little Gaddesden

This village straggles along the borders of Ashridge Park (NT; see Countryside: Country Parks), and a long strip of green has some fine specimen trees of oaks and chestnuts. Many of the houses are very attractive, some having been carefully adapted from rows of cottages, and many have been designed to look harmonious in their woodland setting. It is worth looking in the church of St Peter and St Paul to see the Bridgewater memorials (see Bridgewater Memorial in Heritage: Other Historic Buildings) and the lovely sculpture by Westmacott showing a country family. Ashridge House (see Heritage: Historic Houses) is nearby and probably supplied employment in bygone days. Like Great Gaddesden, Little Gaddesden was often used by the artist Gordon Beningfield as the background for his wildlife paintings.

Little Hadham

Further up the valley of the River Ash than Much Hadham, this village is more scattered, and there are fine views from the churchyard (see Heritage: Churches) to the W and N, towards Albury. The manor house was given to the monks of Ely by King Edgar, and the Capel family, earls of Essex, have been among the landlords. Little Hadham Hall is now a school. It is a handsome Tudor brick building with mullioned windows and a central gateway between towers. A corridor inside this house is 135 feet long. A war memorial stands on the village green.

Little Hormead

Only a short distance away from its sister village, Great Hormead, this village is even smaller. The extensive ironwork on the door of the church (see Heritage: Churches) is famous. Ballon's Farm is a 17th-century building with timber framework and a thatched roof.

Much Hadham

This is a large and popular village with a very attractive main street and a mixture of houses of many different types of architecture. Lying in the valley of the River Ash amid good farming country, it has not been spoiled by modern urban development. The sister of the designer William Morris lived in the 16th-century cottage called Morris Cottage, which is half-timbered and jettied (the upper floor projected beyond the building line of the ground floor). To the N of the church (see Heritage:

Churches) is a plain gabled house now made into flats. This was once a palace of the bishops of London, and it was here that the father of King Henry VII, Edmund Tudor, was born. A leafy lane winds behind the main street beside the river as far as Hadham Cross. In a census of 1851, 52 tradesmen and shopkeepers were among the heads of households in this village.

Newnham

This is a small village set in the rolling countryside of N Hertfordshire. There are some good brasses in the small church (see Arts and Crafts: Brass-Rubbing). There is also a memorial to a local historian, Reginald Hine, who was born in 1883 at Newnham Hall. This is in the form of a tapestry, worked in Tudor style in 1949.

The Pelhams

There are 3 Pelham villages north of the valley where the River Ash rises. At the time of the Domesday Book they were a single estate belonging to the Bishop of London.

Brent Pelham takes its name from the manner in which the land was cleared for cultivation: Brent = burnt. It was destroyed by fire during the reign of Henry I (1100–1135). There are stocks near the church of St Mary (see Heritage: Churches), one of the only 2 sets to survive in this county (the others are at Aldbury). Half a mile NE of the village is Chamberlain's Moat, where pieces of Roman burial urns and vessels were found. The Hall where they now are is a fine Elizabethan house. Brent Pelham is the place where the legendary Piers Shonkes slew a dragon. The Devil was so cross with him that he swore to have Piers' 'body and soul, whether buried within the church or out'. His tomb can be seen, within an alcove in the church wall, located there so as to thwart the Devil's intentions (see Heritage: Churches).

Stocking Pelham is so named because the land was cleared for farming by felling the trees, and the removal of their stocks, or stumps. Many of the houses were made from these logs. It is the smallest of the 3 villages. The public house, the Cock, is thatched and weather-boarded, as many buildings are in Essex. The Old Rectory and the Hall nearby are both moated.

Furneaux Pelham takes its name from the Norman family who owned it, des Furneaux. The motto on the church clock has an interesting inscription (see Heritage: Churches). The village used to have its own brewery, Rayments, but this ceased to function in 1987.

Pirton

A short distance away from the Icknield Way, this village has many fine houses, among them a 17th-century gabled farm, of brick and timber, and an Elizabethan manor house, of stone, with mullioned windows. On the Bedfordshire border, close by, is Pirton Grange, a half-timbered courtyard house with a moat and with a gate-house still standing. There is an interesting church, and excavations in the cemetery show evidence of habitation in the early Iron Age. There are many earthworks here, round the site of the Norman castle.

Redbourn

It is recorded that cricket was played on the village green here as long ago as 1666, the earliest such report in the county. It is still played on the common, a fine triangle bordered by ancient trees and some beautiful houses. The most elegant of these is Cumberland House. Built in 1745, it has now sadly been blighted by office extensions. Aerial photography has established that there was an Iron Age settlement W of the present village. The Romans built Watling Street a mile to the E of this, but the Saxons settled around the site where the parish church now stands. This is of Norman origin, and the carved oak rood screen is very elaborate and fine. There are some good brasses (see Arts and Crafts: Brass-Rubbing). When Watling Street became an important staging-post, many fine houses were built alongside the road, and some of these survive, notably the Priory, which is now office accommodation, and the Red House. The former was built on the site of a medieval priory where in 1178 bones were found which were said to be those of an associate of St Alban, though there is no reliable record to show that he ever existed at all. A bypass has now diverted through traffic, and the village has reverted to its former peaceful character.

Reed

Although there is no evidence to suggest that Reed was ever a Roman settlement, the way in which it has been set out in a grid pattern, with roads at right angles to each other, suggests that the Romans may have had a hand in its design. Set on rolling farmland in the N of the county, most of the manorial houses were on the warm S-facing slopes, and the common land on those facing N. There is a chalkpit which is a nature reserve. The parish church is at the S end of the village. The Norman N doorway has been bricked up. All the angles at the corners of the church are alternate long and short dressed stones, or quoins. It is said that Ely Cathedral can be seen from the N of the village on a clear day.

Sandon

The ancient manor of this village, set 500 feet high, belonged to Saxon kings. Athelstan gave 10 houses in the village to St Paul's, and the cathedral chapter built the church which stands at the top of the village green behind a 16th-century house with an overhanging upper storey. The church tower has brick buttresses. E of the village is a small hillock covered with trees which was probably a defensive mound in the 13th century.

Sarratt

This village has extended well beyond the long green at

the centre. There is a big pond at one end with a public house, the Cricketers, nearby, often used as a backdrop for films and television productions. Cricket is not played on the village green, however, and the village cricket pitch is tucked out of sight at the bottom of King George IV Way. There are some almshouses built in 1821, next to the 12th-century church of Holy Cross, some distance S and W of the village and overlooking the lovely valley of the River Chess. Many flint-and-brick cottages border the green, and there is still a village shop. Dawes Lane, leading off the green, takes you down past Ward's Nursery to Sarratt Bottom, a beautiful valley alongside the Chess. The road passes some remote and attractive old cottages and winds round to take you back to the village. Two other public houses, the Boot, on the village green, and the Cock, near the church, are very popular.

Shenley

This village is known mainly for the presence of the big psychiatric hospital in the vicinity which takes its name from the village and supplies much of the local employment. The centre of the village with its pond and its unusual lock-up (see Heritage: Other Historic Buildings), is very attractive. The parish church in the village was built in 1841, but an older church, which was rebuilt in 1424 and largely dismantled after a disastrous fire in 1753, can still be seen among yew trees at Shenleybury, a little further along the B5378. A lane running into a public footpath leads from Shenleybury to Salisbury Hall, with a museum in its grounds (see Heritage: Museums). Legend has it that this was the place where King Charles II visited Nell Gwynne. He rewarded the man who bought and rebuilt the hall for him with a baronetcy. There is a very attractive public house called Pinks along Rectory Lane (see Eating and Drinking).

Standon

There used to be a weekly market and a fair twice a year in the very wide street that runs through this village. There are a variety of old buildings in the curve of the High Street. The church is unusual because the tower is separate from the rest of the building. The importance of the village in medieval days stems from the presence then of the Command of the Order of St John of Jerusalem with its associated hospice and school. It is not certain which of the old buildings, including the one which was the village school, may have been used by the Knights of St John. At Standon Green End, on the W side of the A10, you can see the Balloon Stone, a boulder of sandstone marking the spot where the first balloon flight in Britain ended in 1784. A brass plate on the stone commemorates the landing, and opposite Knoll Farm a public footpath leads to it. Modern housing now joins the village to Puckeridge.

Therfield

This village is high on the downs, with open views over the adjoining farmland. There is a small green and some attractive old houses including the former manor house which is now the rectory. The church beside it was rebuilt in 1878, and beside that is the site of a village fortification from the 13th century. There are some fine beechwoods on the summit of Therfield Heath, which is a nature reserve because of the plants on the chalky soil. Aerial photographs have shown that there were longbarrows and roundbarrows (mounds of earth made in ancient times to cover one or more burials) on the golf course occupying part of the Heath (see Heritage: Archaeological Sites).

Westmill

This is a very small village, and it is quite unspoilt by modern development and busy roads. Attractive houses are spaced round the village green, on which a summer fête is held biennially. There is an attractive row of cottages behind the parish church, which has Saxon origins. A short distance away is the cottage given to Charles Lamb by his godmother, Sarah. He probably gave it the fanciful name Button Snap. He lived there in 1816, and it is marked by a plaque outside. There is a lane just beyond this cottage leading to the deserted village of Wakeley. This now consists of only one farmhouse but in medieval times may have had a much bigger population.

Weston

The hills round are crowned with beech trees. The village is composed of a tiny green and a tiny pond on which there are ducks. The houses and cottages are varied and attractive. Some parts of the church are of Norman construction, but much of it was rebuilt in the 19th century. There is a Country Museum and Craft Centre at Howell's Farm, nearby (see Heritage: Museums).

Wheathampstead

Modern housing estates have greatly enlarged this village on the River Lee. There was an Iron Age Hill fort here once, and Devil's Dyke, a 40-foot-deep ditch, can still be seen (see Heritage: Archaeological Sites). The parish church is beautiful and has many local associations and some good brasses (see Arts and Crafts: Brass-Rubbing). There are still some fine houses: Mackerye End is a fine sight when the daffodils are in bloom, and Waterend House, built about 1610, is next to the River Lee. Its big barn was removed to St Albans and is used as a restaurant. Juniper bushes grow on the common at Gustard Wood, and there is a nature trail on Nomansland Common (see Countryside).

Widford

The church's W tower has a copper spire. There is a grand doorway in the red-brick churchyard wall, which is a remnant of an Elizabethan house, Widfordbury. This is now a big farm, with a house built in the 17th century. There are many associations with Charles Lamb in Hertfordshire, and especially here, where he stayed with his grandmother, Mary Field, who was housekeeper at Blakesware, which was on the other side of the River Ash but was demolished while he was still alive. His essay 'Blakesmoor' describes the pastoral beauty of the old house and its environment.

Select Bibliography

AA Book of British Villages (Drive Publications, 1980)

AA Country Towns and Villages of Britain (Drive Publications, 1985)

Bagley, A., *Hertfordshire Walks for Motorists* (Warne Gerard, 1982)

Cockman, F.G., *Discovering Preserved Railways* (Shire Publications, 1985)

Cycling in Herts (Sports Council, 1983)

Filler, Roger, *Let's Go With Children in Herts and Beds* (Cube Publications, 1988)

Gardens of England and Wales (National Gardens Scheme, Annual)

Hertfordshire Chain Walk (Herts Footpath Society, 1987)

Hertfordshire County Handbook (The British Publishing Co Ltd, Gloucester, n.d.)

Jones, Arthur, *Shire County Guide. Hertfordshire* (Shire Publications, 1988)

Lands, Neil, *A Visitor's Guide to the Chilterns*

Meadows, Eric G., *Pictorial Guide to Hertfordshire* (White Crescent Press, n.d.)

Moynihan, Liz, *Hertfordshire Rambles* (Countryside Books, 1988)

Pevsner, N., and Cherry, B., *Buildings of England. Hertfordshire* (Penguin, 1977)

Pigram, Ron, *Discovering Walks in the Chilterns* (Shire Publications, 1982)

Pigram, Ron, *Discovering Walks in Hertfordshire* (Shire Publications, 1985)

Slade, H. Gordon, and Richardson, Sir A.E., *Hertfordshire Churches* (Collins, n.d.)

Tompkins, Herbert W., *Highways and Byways in Hertfordshire* (Macmillan, 1926)

Walks in Dacorum (Dacorum Borough Council, 1986)

Where to Go in the Thames and Chilterns (Thames and Chilterns Tourist Board, Annual)

Where to Shop in the Thames and Chilterns (Thames and Chilterns Tourist Board, n.d.)

Winbolt, S.E., *The Chilterns and the Thames Valley* (G. Bell & Sons, 1932)

——, *Penguin Guide to Herts and Bucks* (Penguin, 1949)

Index